D1013579

the
50

GREATEST
BIKE RIDES
OF THE WORLD

IN ASSOCIATION WITH
TIMPSON

GREATEST
BIKE RIDES
OF THE WORLD

SARAH WOODS

Published in the UK in 2016 by
Icon Books Ltd, Omnibus Business Centre,
39–41 North Road, London N7 9DP
email: info@iconbooks.com
www.iconbooks.com

Sold in the UK, Europe and Asia
by Faber & Faber Ltd, Bloomsbury House,
74–77 Great Russell Street,
London WC1B 3DA or their agents

Distributed in the UK, Europe and Asia
by Grantham Book Services, Trent Road,
Grantham NG31 7XQ

Distributed in Australia and New Zealand
by Allen & Unwin Pty Ltd,
PO Box 8500, 83 Alexander Street,
Crows Nest, NSW 2065

Distributed in South Africa by
Jonathan Ball, Office B4, The District,
41 Sir Lowry Road, Woodstock 7925

Distributed in India by Penguin Books India,
7th Floor, Infinity Tower – C, DLF Cyber City,
Gurgaon 122002, Haryana

Distributed in Canada by Publishers Group Canada,
76 Stafford Street, Unit 300, Toronto, Ontario M6J 2S1

Distributed in the USA by Publishers Group West,
1700 Fourth Street, Berkeley, CA 94710

ISBN: 978-178578-181-0

Images – see individual pictures

Typeset and designed by Simmons Pugh

Printed and bound in the UK by Clays Ltd, St Ives plc

ABOUT THE AUTHOR

S arah Woods is the author of over a dozen travel books, a fellow of the Royal Geographical Society and a member of the British Guild of Travel Writers. She has won the prestigious BGTW 'Travel Guide Writer of the Year' award and has twice won the Kenneth Westcott Jones Award. As a travel presenter on British daytime TV, Sarah won the PSA prize for reportage in 2012. She is also the author of *The 50 Greatest Road Trips of the World* in this series.

CONTENTS

Asia

Australasia

The Americas

Africa

INTRODUCTION

Though many men from umpteen nations throughout history have laid claim to the invention of the bicycle – including, somewhat bizarrely, Leonardo da Vinci – it was Englishman John Kemp Starley who created the cycle in the form we recognise today. His design, a bicycle with a chain-driven rear wheel and a steerable front wheel, was patented in 1885 and set the Victorian era's two-wheel craze in motion. Soon, cycling had not only revolutionised transport but also our clothing – bloomers (long knickers that tapered above the knee) arose from the popularity of pushbikes with women. Indeed, the bicycle became a symbol for the suffragette movement for the freedom it offered.

Since then, the bicycle has gone through a variety of design trends, including racing styles with dropped handlebars, chunky mountain bikes with robust, balloon tyres and light-as-a-feather speed machines made from carbon-fibre frames. Be it for excitement, necessity, adventure or relaxation, two-wheeling today is enjoyed all over the world by people of all ages. Few things stick in a young child's memory more than the day they can finally ride a bicycle without wobbling. Within a couple of years they are relishing the adrenaline thrills that bikes offer. By the time they are teens, a bike is invaluable for the independence it brings. As adults, we cycle to work, for leisure or as sport to keep us fit. In our later years, cycling provides us with a gentle mode of transport at a slower pace.

Freewheeling through tufted French vineyards, scaling rocky, cloud-topped tracks in the Himalayas, rattling past whitewashed sugar-cube houses in narrow Spanish valleys, surviving the peaks of the Yorkshire Dales and the volcanoes of Colombia and tackling truly hair-raising descents in rural Cuba: the sheer variety of routes in *The 50 Greatest Bike Rides of the World* will have you reaching for your cycle clips, helmet and gloves. Enjoy tales of scenic single tracks, switchback climbs and routes newly discovered – it's time to get those panniers packed and sprockets checked and climb into the saddle!

THE 50 GREATEST
BIKE RIDES OF THE WORLD

UNITED KINGDOM AND IRELAND

BELFAST, NORTHERN IRELAND

For decades, the city of Belfast wasn't characterised by its fine architecture but more for its security barricades. During the worst of 'the troubles', amid bullets, guns and bombs, Belfast symbolised a city riven by fear, hatred and sectarian clashes. Today, now that the 50 years of unrest and social conflict is consigned to the history books, Belfast and its slogan-daubed mural-painted walls, vast expanses of terraced houses and high brick walls topped by reinforced steel panels have become as much as a part of the city's historical fabric as its grand Edwardian mansions, Victorian landmarks, Georgian buildings, sculptures and state-of-the-art modern structures. Gentrified docklands, swish quayside apartments and chichi wine bars, loungers and bistros rub shoulders with giant fortified police stations not far from the violent flashpoints of the 1970s that made the bulletins of the world's prime-time TV news. Billions of euros have been pumped into the local economy from an impressive roll-call of international investors – and it shows. Mature leafy parks, elegant plazas and pedestrianised shopping zones attract large numbers of tourists. Nature reserves, museums, literary and socio-political attractions do a roaring trade. Ancestry tours – a far-reach phenomenon that draws anyone with a drop of Irish blood – are booming. As a 21st-century city, Belfast is modern, welcoming and

Photo: Gallodapez

handsome and determined not to be stigmatised by walls that once kept communities apart.

Another big change for Belfast is its move to become increasingly cycle-friendly. In recent years, a sizeable network of cycle lanes, off-road paths and riverside terraces have encouraged more people to explore the city on two wheels. A favourite route is the Comber Greenway: a seven-mile (eleven-kilometre) traffic-free section of the National Cycle Network that runs along the disused Belfast to Comber railway line. A tranquil green corridor that offers great views of the famous Parliament buildings at Stormont, Scrabo Tower and the Belfast Hills, the route opened in 2008 and has a number of access points, including Dee Street (close to the Harland & Wolff shipyard), the C.S. Lewis Statue at Holywood Arches, Bloomfield Walkway, Tullycarnet and Dundonald. Community training projects have helped set up groups that offer bike maintenance and Belfast's annual event calendar now includes a wide-range of cycling activities. An extension to the route now links Comber Greenway to the Titanic Quarter and other existing riverside trails into the city centre. Not purely a tourist boon, the route also enables East Belfast residents to get around without needing a car: not just to the city, but also out into the open countryside and beyond.

The old railway line that Comber Greenway runs along closed in 1950 and is full of wildlife. At Dundonald the route diverts briefly from the old track to a section of riverside path to Millmount Road before continuing to Comber through a rural landscape, passing the Billy Neill (MBE) Soccer Centre of Excellence with views of adjacent farmland and Scrabo Tower. Cyclists and walkers can cross the River Enler and farm lanes using a number of reinstated bridges before arriving at Comber. Visiting cyclists arrive in Belfast with their bikes to venture along this trail using the train stations of Belfast Central, Bridge End and Sydenham. Bicycles are carried free of charge as long as travel is after 9.30am Monday to Friday.

Although the pathway is wide and entirely off road (with no stiles), there are junctions where the route crosses main roads. All of Belfast's tourist information offices carry the Comber Greenway Leaflet and National Cycle Network Map 99, while the Northern Ireland Tourist Board has a downloadable guide (www.discovernorthernireland.com) that includes tips for safe and enjoyable urban cycling and details of other cycling routes in Belfast.

Easily navigated from either direction, popular opinion seems united on which way to journey the Comber Greenway – most consider it a more scenic route from a Comber start. Either way has pros and cons, but I tend to agree with the majority. You can either join a small group for a Belfast bike tour (there are several specialist outfits) or do it solo: it's a straightforward seven-mile (eleven-kilometre) run along fairly well-signed paths.

From the town centre, go north out of the square on Mill Street, take a right at the first roundabout and follow the road until just before it joins the main road to Belfast – the start of the Comber Greenway is signed from here. From the very beginning, the pathway ventures through picturesque countryside with views of Scrabo Tower, the 125-foot (38-metre) turreted Northern Irish landmark built in 1857, where Universal Pictures filmed scenes for its movie *Dracula Untold*. Surrounded by a lush patchwork of green-and-yellow arable fields, the pathway meanders gently for a mile or so, crossing roads and sloping up and down until it reaches a large white church. Take the bridge to the left and head towards a pedestrian crossing before climbing the steps up the hill where a blue 'National Cycle Route 99' sign leads to another traffic-free stretch of the route. Enjoy a couple more miles of rural splendour before nearing Belfast, when the route passes a few more major roads.

At Holywood Arches take time to admire 'The Searcher', a bronze statue of a man peering into a wardrobe and a fine memorial to C.S. Lewis, the Ulsterman who is best known for writing *The Lion, the Witch and the Wardrobe*. Clive Staples Lewis (1898–1963) held academic positions at both Oxford University (1925–54) and Cambridge University (1954–63) and was a close friend of J.R.R. Tolkien. Although he was schooled in Hertfordshire, Lewis grew up in Northern Ireland: his family home, 'Little Lea', is in the Strandtown area of East Belfast. Once you've passed the statue, the end of the route is at Dee Street – a rather unprepossessing place whose best feature is a 'Comber Greenway' information board pointing out what you've just seen. From here, a bridge crosses over the Sydenham bypass and leads to the wide boulevard of Sydenham Road, the mammoth entertainment complex 'The Odyssey' and the River Lagan with its canals, towpaths, wetlands, meadows and mixed woodlands. Follow the river to the left and pass over Lagan Weir or take the downstream path through to the newly developed Titanic Quarter to see where the fateful RMS *Titanic* was built in 1909.

Endurance level: Easy

Tip: Be alert to debris on the road and the threat of puncture from thorns, sharp stones and old rusty nails.

Contacts:
Belfast City Bike Tours
www.belfastcitybiketours.com

Belfast Bike Tours
www.belfastbiketours.com

Belfast Tourism
www.visitbelfast.com

ISLE OF MULL, SCOTLAND

Wherever you're coming from, travelling to the Isle of Mull is a journey and a half. For me, it is a ten-hour cross-country drive from the university city of Cambridge in the UK's East Anglia region up to one of Scotland's most beautiful islands. From mountains to moorlands, Mull is an island of wild landscapes trimmed by 300 miles (483 kilometres) of dramatic coastline that are home to some stunning beaches. A pretty harbour town of brightly painted houses is instantly recognisable to children aged ten and younger as Tobermory, the setting for the BBC's children's TV show *Balamory*. Cyclists a good deal older are certain to spot the severity of the terrain before anything else: Mull is a place where eagles soar, winds howl and crashing waves roar, and where a distance of 62 miles (100 kilometres) can feel like ten times more. Yet no other Scottish island offers cyclists such a rich, traffic-free landscape to explore along undulating, complex roads with breathtaking views and abundant wildlife. I defy any cycling nature-fan not to inwardly whoop with glee as they ride the route between Salen and Calgary Bay: a magnificent stretch that provides constant reminders of the awe and wonder of the natural world – otters are a highlight.

From Glasgow, Scotland's largest city situated in the country's West Central Lowlands on the banks of the River Clyde, take a three-hour train to Oban to catch the ferry to Craignure, which on a good day will take just 50 minutes. First-rate planning and preparation are required for any trip to Mull, given the few shops and limited accommodation on the island. It is also worth whispering a prayer to the weather gods. Or maybe two. Or three.

From the ferry dock at Craignure, take the relatively flat road up the north coast to Salen before turning left towards Calgary Bay. The road becomes much more curvaceous along this stretch, rising to a hill before tumbling down towards a crossroads. Here, between the southern loop and the northern loop of Isle of Mull, on the picturesque south coast, I'm certain an equal number of cyclists turn left as turn right. For me, the northern loop to the right is my route of choice for its sheer gape-mouthed beauty. A flat section wiggles out along the sea towards Ulva, offering captivating coastal seascapes that ensure three miles (five kilometres) pass in a flash. Then suddenly, a sharp steep hill reminds you of Mull's gruelling gradients and takes you approximately 328 feet (100 metres) above sea level overlooking Ulva. These mesmerising Scottish highland views accompany you all the way to Calgary Bay, regularly dipping down to the sea to flatten out for a while before taxing every muscle with a testing series of undulating ridges.

Although part of you wants to yell 'stop, please stop …', the rest of you wants to holler 'wow, this is so much FUN!' – even the descents and ascents that require a fair amount of technical gear-change wizardry. Eventually, you arrive at the foot of the mountain that marks a climb to one of the most potentially nerve-wracking descents down to Calgary Bay. If you survive the fast-paced downhill stretch without incident, due to the wayward sheep that amble and scramble along the road, you'll make it to the cyclist-friendly bar at the Calgary Bay Hotel, where you'll undoubtedly deserve a stiff a drink.

From Calgary to Dervaig, the route passes through dense forest that obscures the views towards the islands to the west, but it redeems itself with a fine, fearsome mountain climb over to Tobermory. From the top, a splendid far-reaching vista reveals a 'surprise' – an even steeper climb up ahead. After pounding the pedals into a deep valley, the ascent requires a considerable amount of blood, sweat and tears: that there is no second 'surprise' is a godsend as you flop to the ground on your knees.

At this point, with good reason, Tobermory's whisky distillery will look mightily inviting to cyclists with parched lips and legs like jelly. This is the home of fine single malt and tours run regularly with plenty of opportunity for visitors to take a wee dram. After such a punishing ascent, the vertical drop through the streets of Tobermory is a journey of pure joy. Colour and charm add to the exhilaration of arriving at the real-life setting of *Balamory*!

From Tobermory, the uphill road to Salen pushes up the rugged north coast to a magical summit before rolling down towards the sea to level off before entering Salen. The single-track roads then get progressively narrower. Looking for a nice, short 'out and back'? Then head from Tobermory to Aros Park. Considered the fabulous back garden for the town of Tobermory. Trails begin at the distillery and meander through woodlands strewn with ferns and past waterfalls, BBQ grills and fishing lakes. Superb views also roll back to Tobermory and over the Sound of Mull to the craggy face of Ardnamurchan. On the edge of the site, there's a spectacular look-out at Alainn View up into the tree tops. For cycle-friendly accommodation run by cycling nuts who help guests to plan routes, book an overnight stay at the Garden Lodge. Not only do they serve enormous man-sized Scottish breakfasts, they also have a large porch area for stowing bikes and wet gear. Small tour groups and one-to-one rides are offered by guide Simon Bartle, a British Cycling Qualified Mountain Bike Leader, who runs tailored half, full and multi-day mountain bike and cyclocross tours of the Isle of Mull and the Morvern peninsula. Simon is also a professional bike mechanic and can offer advice if you are looking to purchase a new bike for riding on Mull. He also knows of plenty of secret places for adventure-loving cyclists that aren't obvious on a map.

Endurance level: Moderate–Difficult

Tip: Save plenty of energy for a final push on the last peak – it's a satisfying slow-burn with a steep crest as a finale.

Contacts:
Explore Mull
www.isle-of-mull.net

Isle of Mull Cycling Club
www.isleofmullcyclingclub.co.uk

Tobermory Isle of Mull
www.tobermory.co.uk

BEALACH NA BÀ, SCOTLAND

The awe-inspiring scenery of the Scottish Highlands can humble mere cycling mortals: the hush of still, silent roads and the enormity of the peaks are humility for the soul. Superb trails lay knitted together by tangled tufts of foliage in some of the most remarkable unspoiled scenery in rural Europe. These rugged wilderness qualities have earned Scotland a reputation as one of the best places in the world to mountain bike along a web of rugged trails into extraordinary backcountry. Lots of route options are based around the National Cycling Network in the wildest parts of Scotland, with an unbeatable, bracing wind-in-the-hair ride across the mountains of the Applecross Peninsula to the Bealach na Bà (Pass of the Cattle) involving a monster road-climb of more than 2,050 feet (625 metres): a route that's notorious for its jaw-dropping views and its utterly terrifying bends.

The Bealach's undisputed king of road climbs span the pass from sea level to summit in just six miles (ten kilometres). To many cyclists across the UK, it is the Holy Grail of hillclimbs and home to a sell-out cycling event every year. Voted by National Geographic as one of the world's greatest road trips, Bealach in Wester Ross is an epic challenge in which man and bike are united in agony and ecstasy. At just under 44 miles (70 kilometres), dedicated amateurs have clocked it up in around three hours – but don't be surprised if it takes a great deal longer. Fill your lungs with pure Scottish air, slip into the lowest gear and prepare for the burn after a short, sharp, power burst. Reaching 20 per cent at its steepest gradient, this mostly single-track route has one redeeming feature, other than ensuring the ultimate riding challenge: it is home

Photo: Stefan Krause

to the superb kitchen at the Applecross Inn, a much deserved past winner of the award for Bar Food Pub of the Year. But to dine on fine pub grub, you must first survive the climb, which is a near-religious experience with shades of the opening scene of Herzog's film *Aguirre, The Wrath of God*. Snaking up the mountainside, with golden sun lighting up the glen on one side and a blanket of mist across the hill on the other, is not unlike a trip to the pearly gates – except Bealach na Bà has hairpin bends and joyous swooping descents.

A number of extremely professional mountain bike tour operators run bespoke tours to Bealach na Bà for individual riders, small groups and bigger organised trips – from mellow ambles through the country lanes to iconic coast-to-coast adventures. Every level of rider will feel the buzz of the quietude and splendour of Scotland's off-the-beaten-track. It doesn't matter if you feel like an easy pedal or prefer to embark on a challenging battle with the highest UK mountain roads. Along the way, riders stay in carefully selected guest houses and small hotels, so that after riding during the day there is plenty of opportunity to relax in the evenings. Everyone has the freedom to explore and enjoy at their own pace. Of course, solo rides without a guide can be arranged with the aid of a decent map. Some are offered with detailed route notes so that it simplifies preparation – there are even suggested designated stops along the way at great places to eat, drink, rest and absorb the views. Other Highlands tour firms will transfer luggage between overnight accommodation to ensure a lightweight and care-free ride.

Speeds faster than 30 miles per hour (48 kilometres per hour) are rarely permitted on the Bealach na Bà, much like on the great mountain passes of the Swiss Alps. The constant switching back and forth on perilously tight corkscrew bends, and the ridiculously slim width of the road at the succession of 'passing places' adds a constant threat of jeopardy. One ominous signpost provides an insight of what you're letting yourself in for, reading: 'Applecross Road normally impassable in wintry conditions. Road to Applecross (Bealach Na Bà). This road rises to a height of 2,053 feet with gradients of 1 in 5 and hairpin bends. Not advised for learner drivers, very large vehicles or caravans after first mile.'

GULP.

Rather sneakily, the road starts off climbing nice and gently, lulling you into thoughts of 'hey, this is easier than I thought'. Then it gets steeper, much steeper. Suddenly steeper. Then even steeper still. On and on and on, with yet another hairpin bend. Then, just as you think it may be ready to level out, the real climb really starts. It hurts, a lot, so much that most ordinary folk would get off and walk. There's a chill in the air, even in the height of summer, and once the mist starts to thicken you know the end is nigh. Reaching the clouds at the top brings relief and a real sense of triumph – and if the clouds are wispy, breathtaking views of the isles of Raasay and Skye.

Nothing compares to the gleeful roller-coaster descent with the wind on your back – you will give thanks a thousand times over for the invention of the bike. Your self-esteem will have soared as high as the mountain. You'll feel braver, bigger and wear a grin as broad as a Cheshire cat.

Expert guides that run tours in remote Highland regions hold the respected Mountain Bike Leader qualification and have years of experience riding the backcountry trails of Scotland. They are also clued up about technical bike maintenance, have plenty of mountain bike yarns to share and are savvy about the culture and history of the unique Scottish Highlands. Expect plenty of jokes, lots of camaraderie and a constant supply of energy bars, bananas and chia seeds.

Endurance level: Difficult

Tip: Pack a pair of binoculars for this trip – the sight of a rare golden eagle is not to be missed.

Contacts:
Visit Scotland
www.visitscotland.com

Wester Ross
www.visitwester-ross.com

SNOWDONIA, WALES

Snowdon, in rock-strewn North Wales, is often cited as one of the true 'must-do' routes of British adventure cycling: a trail that takes riders up the highest mountain in England and Wales. And while a voluntary ban excludes cycles from the mountain in the busiest summer months, in the low season (October to April), Llanberis – the only practical route for someone prepared to tackle all 3,560 feet of it on bike – is ready to ride. There are shorter routes to the top of the mountain, but the Llanberis path is a lengthy five-mile (eight-kilometre) slog: it looks mean on a map, and even tougher up close. Not all of it is rideable and on an overcast day (of which there are plenty in lush, green Wales) the roads glisten with water as swollen beads of sweat form a band along the brow.

Terrifying views of the north-west flanks of Snowdon taunt cyclists in the foothills by gradually disappearing into layers of cloud: it's like a visual metaphor for being permanently unreachable. However, once the mountain railway station is far behind, the climb up steep tarmac is confirmation that, ready or not, you're on your way to the obscured summit. The going is slow; more of a climb-and-crawl than a true uphill. It's impossible not to wobble as you try not to mow down a pair of hillwalkers. The grass is tussocky, the asphalt is looking like it is about to peter out and it takes loads of self-confidence not to turn around and look back down the track. The climb proper begins when there are more rocks than road and needs navigating with skill. Hit the path wrong, on a slippery stretch, and you'll need to dismount and sling your bike up on your shoulder. Sections call for some daring, but with such a challenging climb ahead it pays the wise man to play it safe. A fall, a bump, a cut or serious damage (to a limb or the bike) and it's a heck of a long limp back down.

After a particularly tough series of pointed ridges topped by a patch of sprouting, tangled turf, the half-way station café should be in sight. Half way, according to the map, is at a height of around 1,740 feet (530 metres) – a lofty achievement that deserved to be celebrated with an iced bun and a big mug of tea. Alas, it is shut for winter. Bleak, deserted and with boards across the windows, it is a long way from the cheery place that serves warm muffins, ice creams and chocolate cake in the sunnier months. Below me, the mists clear for a second or two and it dawns on me how far I've come – and how far I've yet to manage. Pushing on, with a swig of water, I climb back into the saddle. It is getting steeper and steeper and more and more slippery and the rocks are doubling in size. It's a scramble, and an undignified one at that, as I skid and trip across the boulders

Photo: Berit

in thickening mist. Bruised and battered, I admit that the route is no longer remotely rideable and stumble into the clouds, dragging my bike. It is gloomy, damp and I'm not far from an exposed ridge, but everything beyond that is invisible. Spooky shadows loom up ahead as I lug myself and the bike across a formidable ridge of frost-shattered rocks and aim for a huge monolith beyond.

Could it be? Yes it is! Thank goodness that I studied the map before my ascent. The finger of stone rising up the north-west flank of the mountain means I'm close to the summit – it's a landmark for another trail. Buoyed by the news, I climb back on my bike and ride the rest of the way: fearless in my gear choices and pumped full of bravado. By the time my head pops through the canopy of thick mist, I realise I'm in the company of walkers: all of us have gritted our teeth and dug deep for the final stretch and have barely noticed it is raining too. Pushing the bike up the final stretch, I try my best not to wipe out anyone gasping for breath on foot and claim a selfie with the big marker stone. I spot a sign for the Snowdon Ranger path, the other bike-legal route to the summit and wonder how it compares to Llanberis. After momentarily toying with the idea of taking it for the descent, I opt to play it safe on the basis that I don't want to fall foul of Snowdon's abrupt abysses in the poor light. I've heard of competent cyclists who have lost confidence when they've encountered poor visibility. It doesn't take much for panic to set in – and I'm mindful that it is a long way to the nearest A&E from the top of a mountain.

The route down is wet and slippery, but relatively undemanding, as I weave my way through a gaggles of walkers and rocks. Wider strips of path covered in loose rocks of various sizes lead to skinny bumpy sections with cobbles. Some tighter stretches, layered in uneven slabs that have formed a rocky staircase, are almost entirely covered by slimy moss. When I find it tricky to see, I let out a whoop and holler at the rocks through the swirling mist as I fear battering someone with my bike on the way down.

By the time I arrive at the bottom, rain-soaked and hungry, I've used all my water, eaten all my snacks and made full use of my map and suitable clothing. I estimate I rode about 75 per cent of the climb (pushing a bike up the steepest bits makes a lightweight model a sensible option) and about 40 per cent of the descent. There are lots of stretches where injury is a major risk but this tough short ride doesn't need to be dangerous: pick a quiet time, dismount anywhere that's slippery or a death-drop and proceed with care and consideration for others.

A voluntary ban on mountain biking on Snowdon comes into effect between 10am and 6pm from 1 May to 30 September each year. It's been agreed with The Snowdonia National Park, Gwynedd County Council, Cyclists' Touring Club, Welsh Cycling Union and International Mountain Bicycling Association as a safety precaution due to the sheer number of summer walkers. Restrictions were first introduced more than twenty years ago to prevent speeding bikers colliding with walkers, so cyclists either need to get their Snowdon fix October to April or to start out early morning October to May.

Endurance level: Difficult

Tip: Pack a head torch to prepare for poor visibility should low cloud descend.

Contacts:
Snowdonia Mountains and Coast

www.visitsnowdonia.info

Cycling North Wales
www.cyclingnorthwales.co.uk

THE WAY OF THE ROSES, ENGLAND

Since opening in 2010, the Way of the Roses has positioned itself nicely as the UK's newest and most exciting coast-to-coast cycling trip. Plenty of big hills attract flocks of dedicated hill riders, while stretches of unmade dirt offers enough challenging off-road sections to keep the mountain bike crowd thrilled. Passing through both the red rose county of Lancashire and the white rose county of Yorkshire, the Way of the Roses links the seafront of Morecambe on the Irish Sea coast with the North Sea coast at Bridlington 170 miles (274 kilometres) to the east. From beautiful shorelines and historical market towns to underground caverns, bizarre rock formations and rolling hills, this well-signed route offers cycling flexibility – do it in two to five days or take a more relaxed pace as either a guided or independent holiday. Most cyclists travel west to east to take full advantage of a gusty tailwind. However you tackle it, instantly recognisable red and white roses lead the way, making the route easy to follow in either direction along a wide variety of terrain along traffic-free paths, on-road cycle lanes, country lanes and quieter roads.

As National Cycle Network Route 69, the Way of the Roses was commissioned to celebrate fifteen years of the National Cycle Network. Good rail connections at both Morecambe and Bridlington make arriving with a bike at either end of each trail incredibly straightforward. From Morecambe the route winds to Lancaster, Settle, Cracoe, Pateley Bridge, Ripon, Boroughbridge, York, Pocklington, Driffield and Bridlington, crossing the rugged northern part of the red rose county of Lancashire, before then advancing over a broad stretch of Yorkshire, the white rose county. Ranking high among Britain's most stunning countryside and fascinating heritage sites, highlights on the route include such areas as the Lune Valley, the Forest of Bowland Area of Outstanding Natural Beauty (AONB), Yorkshire Dales National Park, Nidderdale AONB, the Vale of York and the Yorkshire Wolds. The Fountains Abbey and Studley Royal World Heritage Site near Ripon makes a great rest stop as do the attractions of the historic city of York. A tailor-made website for the route details each section with grade information, sightseeing suggestions and a rough estimate of how long it will take. The hills start after about eight miles (thirteen kilometres) and the biggest climbs are between Settle and Brimham Rocks (a few miles east of Pateley Bridge), roughly between miles 35 and 65 (kilometres 56 and 104).

Those travelling west to east will find the hardest hills are the succession of peaks between Settle and Brimham Rocks, with the slog out of Settle the toughest challenge. Riding east to west, the hardest section is climbing Greenhow Hill out of Pateley Bridge – Greenhow is the highest point at a whopping 1,312 feet (402 metres) above sea level! A tradition is to snap a triumphant 'I've survived' selfie next to a Way of Roses board for posterity at either end.

English history books tell the stories of the Wars of the Roses: a series of bloody civil wars fought in medieval England between 1455 and 1487. For 32 years, a bitter struggle for the English throne was waged between two branches of the

Photo: Kreuzschnabel

same family, the House of York and the House of Lancaster, both descended from Edward III. The battles began in 1455, fuelled by a building resentment of the way the Lancaster family had seized the throne in 1399. The struggle for power was known as the War of the Roses because the Lancaster emblem was a red rose and the York emblem a white rose. Battle followed battle and it seemed that the feud would never end. However, when Henry Vll (representing the Lancaster family) married Elizabeth of York (representing the York family), the two families were unified. Henry created the Tudor rose, containing both the White Rose of York and the Red Rose of Lancaster, to symbolise the end to all wars between York and Lancaster. Historians debate the impact the wars had on medieval English life, though it undoubtedly prompted changes in the feudal system because of the many casualties among the nobility and the subsequent increase in the power of the merchant classes that still exists today.

Today, the Way of the Roses route showcases the best that Northern England has to offer – including this rich cultural heritage in an array of museums along the way, including Lancaster Castle, Williamson Park, Parcevall Hall, Fountains Abbey, Ripley Castle, York Minster, Beningbrough Hall and Burton Agnes Hall – all grand palatial English piles of great splendour.

Choose a bike that allows you to carry luggage (if you're not taking advantage of the many baggage transfer services or support vehicle options on offer). A touring or hybrid bike is best for pannier, though tandems, recumbents, hand-cycles and tricycles have all be able to finish this route. Ahead of the notoriously steep hills, give your brakes a thorough check. Cycle shops en route offer repairs, spares and maintenance, but it is worth packing a basic tool kit with spare inner tubes, tyre levers, pump, multi-tool and adjustable spanners.

Sustrans publishes an official route map, even though the route itself is well signed. Food options run from small grocery stores to pubs, cafes and chip shops – the Way of the Roses website has a comprehensive list of places to eat and buy snacks. There is also an accommodation section to help with pre-booking cycle-friendly B&Bs and guest houses.

Endurance level: Moderate–Difficult

Tip: Relax and enjoy this breathtaking ride – it's an exhilarating, not exhausting away to take in the gorgeous countryside.

Contacts:
Way of the Roses Cycle Route
www.wayoftheroses.info

Visit Lancashire
www.visitlancashire.com

Welcome to Yorkshire
www.yorkshire.com

OLD MOOR, ENGLAND

Sightseeing in the saddle is one of the best ways to engage with birds and wildlife, so it feels fitting to cycle the Royal Society for the Protection of Birds' (RSPB) Old Moor reserve during the UK's Bike Week in June. This fine natural green space is open to cyclists year-round, providing a chance to explore the wild, open meadows and bird-rich waters of Dearne Valley in any season: when I arrive, in summer, the fertile grasslands are ablaze with colourful butterflies and orchids. I can't wait to two-wheel with nature.

Old growth woodlands pepper these curvaceous moorlands, once scarred by coal mining and heavy industry, and I'm intrigued by the history of the South Yorkshire landscape. As a county, South Yorkshire was formed in 1974, encompassing the boroughs of Barnsley, Doncaster, Rotherham and Sheffield. Developed around the coal and iron industry, parts of the region are known for Sheffield steel, though there are older relics than the abandoned factories and smoke stacks. Cave art and historic artefacts dating back 12,800 years (Palaeolithic period) have been found in Deepcar, North Sheffield. Though the mines closed more than three decades ago, the region remains riddled with deep coal seams. South Yorkshire's Dearne Valley region has benefited from significant regeneration since it was blighted by spoil heaps in the 1980s. Today the terrain comprises a mishmash of rolling farmland, mossy woodlands and former colliery workings, neatly divided by the reed-trimmed River Dearne, old canals and disused railway lines. Oh, and the M1 motorway. Yet for me there is no roar of traffic. No trucks. No service stations. Just me, my bike and the feral joys of nature at the mouth of the 350-mile (563-kilometre) national Trans Pennine Trail cycle route.

My journey begins at Old Moor, a cycle-friendly nature reserve that links the Trans Pennine Trail with four other nature reserves: Wombwell Ings, Gypsy Marsh, Edderthorpe Flash and Bolton Ings. So cyclists with plenty of oomph, take note. Me, I've chosen a rugged 21-mile (34-kilometre) trail from the Old Moor's options; the others are five and thirteen miles (eight and 21 kilometres) – a far cry from the

Photo: Terry Robinson

Photo: Steven Ruffles

whole shebang, but still meaning a full day in the saddle. The glorious sunshine I have pre-ordered arrives on cue. It's hot; in fact, it's positively steamy – a benefit of being shielded from rain-bearing clouds by the Pennines mountain ranges. The valley is perfect for cycling as it has gentle gradients and slowly unfolding scenery with good quality trails. Old Moor, right in the heart of the Dearne Valley, offers skies, fields and open waters teeming with wildlife and birds throughout the year, from newly hatched ducklings, geese and sand martins to great crested grebes, warblers and over 8,000 golden plovers.

Birds, I soon realise, seem less afraid of me in the saddle than when I dismount and approach on foot. Dragonflies dance over wildlife pools, dozens of common blue butterflies flit around and water voles scurry along the banks. In autumn, peregrines soar high above the hedgerows of ripening berries, trees and falling leaves. With panniers secured and sprockets, valves and spokes double-checked, I swerve around a rabbit with a wobble. Old Moor wildlife, here I come!

My syncopated pounding on the pedals produces a comforting rhythmic pulse as one leafy stretch leads to another. I'm so preoccupied with Mother Nature's wonders that the hours slip effortlessly by. Old Moor reserve is awash with colour and I am blessed with stunning views. First I am treated to yellow-green pasture littered with sweet-smelling wildflowers and leaf-shrouded hides. I spot mute swans with a trail of fluffy cygnets in the lakes and numerous common terns among the reed beds and feel wholly in-tune with my surroundings. Now, rather than fretting about my mile-rate, I abandon myself to the landscape. A magnificent marsh orchid heralds my arrival at a particularly secluded, peaceful meadow expanse. I am elated and barely notice a slow-burn in my calves brought on by a rigorous gradual incline. Free from the hubbub of noise pollution, I imbibe the luxury of silence from the ridge and, a little tipsy on tranquillity, revel in the only audible sound; my own breath – a strangely spiritual experience. The moment is lost somewhat when, on spotting a distant roe deer, I drop my jaw and ingest a mouthful of flies. Yet as I add a little-ringed plover, a redshank, a kingfisher, several tree bumblebees, a yellow wagtail, an oystercatcher and a sedge warbler to the list of my day's sightings, my bike, nature and I feel in perfect synchronicity.

The RSPB encourages cycling on reserves where bikes, nature and other visitors can happily co-exist, from freewheeling in the wilds in Scotland and pottering through the lush scenery of Mid Wales to pedalling along the Suffolk coast and riding through Bedfordshire heath and woodlands. Birding by bike is a more environmentally responsible form of transportation than driving to different birdwatching hotspots. Pedal slowly to give yourself more time to observe the habitat and listen out for wildlife and nearby birds. Slow pedalling will also make less noise that could disturb birds – and you'll see more wildlife if you've remembered to oil the chain, seat and pedals to minimise squeaks, rattles and clanks.

Endurance level: Moderate–Difficult

Tip: It pays to stretch and limber up ahead of this ride as it starts with a testing climb.

Contacts:
RSPB Dearne Valley – Old Moor
www.rspb.org.uk

Yorkshire Tourist Board
www.yorkshire.com

THE RIDGEWAY, ENGLAND

Running from Overton Hill in Wiltshire to the curvy Chilterns in Buckinghamshire, the 87-mile (139-kilometre) Ridgeway Trail doesn't – unfortunately – offer cyclists a continuous unbroken ride, as the trail becomes a walkers-only footpath at Goring, east of the River Thames. However, cyclists are ingenious souls who have worked out a solution, using a carefully mapped-out cycling route that follows a mix of bridleways and leafy country lanes. For the initial 43 miles (69 kilometres) of The Ridgeway, the going is cycle-friendly and as one of the UK's National Trails the scenery is suitably grand. Starting near a UNESCO World Heritage Site in Avebury in the Wiltshire countryside and ending in Streatley in Berkshire on the River Thames, the path winds its way through rolling downland and sun-dappled woods, passing the Neolithic barrow and chamber tomb of the Wayland's Smithy and the chalky-white 177-foot (110-metre) prehistoric hill figure, the Uffington White Horse. As you pedal through this ancient landscape, it is impossible not to imagine the legions who have travelled before you since prehistoric times. Herdsmen, armies, farmers and merchants have all trodden The Ridgeway, a route that once formed part of an ancient trading route that stretched from Norfolk to the Dorset coast.

Apart from the stretch to the east of the Thames, The Ridgeway has Byway, Restricted Byway or Bridleway status, all of which can be legally ridden by bike. Once you move away from the trail, particularly in Wiltshire, there are plenty of other ridable paths – mainly on mud, chalk and compacted gravel – that mean you don't need to hit the tarmac for hours.

Over the years, parts of the route have become purposed for different activities, so The Ridgeway varies dramatically along its length, depending on what it's used for, e.g. farm access, recreation or conservation. Near the main points of interest, the trail is busier with families and walkers, but away from these it can be empty and utterly silent. Through this surprisingly remote part of southern central England, the trail winds its way north-easterly over high ground, passing through designated Areas of Outstanding Natural Beauty a world away from any urban distractions.

Only in the Chilterns does The Ridgeway run through villages and small towns, past stone-built tea rooms and cafes. After this, there is a lovely nine-mile (fourteen-kilometre) stretch from Britwell Hill, just west of Watlington to Bledlow, west of Princes Risborough. Cyclists keen to enjoy a long-distance ride east of the Thames to continue the thrill in the style of The Ridgeway have a choice of two good substitute routes to follow: the Swans Way starts at Goring-on-Thames, just across the river from Streatley, and travels to Bledlow, where it turns north away from the line of The Ridgeway. At Bledlow cyclists and horse riders can then join the Icknield Way Riders' Route that provides a good alternative route to The Ridgeway as far as Pitstone Hill, just a couple of miles from Ivinghoe Beacon. As Britain's oldest road, the 5,000-year-old Ridgeway picks through archaeologically rich glades, dells and gentle slopes, with several nature reserves and chalk grassland habitats. The 43-mile (69-kilometre) western half of the route crosses just a few short sections of road and is predominantly a hard stone surface, so can be ridden year-round unless there is heavy snow.

What makes this moderately challenging, visually pleasing route all the more compelling is that it is packed with

historical mementoes, such as the striking hilltop fortresses Barbury Castle, Liddington Castle and Uffington Castle. Another upside is that the terrain is definitely undulating – not hilly. The land isn't flat, but it isn't massively hilly either: none of the hills are enormous so the route is suitable for all abilities.

And a downside? Just be prepared for punctures. The route can get rutty as it starts to dry out after spring. The flint stone found in most chalk hillsides in summer can cut rubber tyres to ribbons, while in winter it can be lethal as it is like riding on polished marble slavered in toothpaste. In some stretches, the signage could be better too, so be sure to have an Ordinance Survey map to hand or a National Trail route map.

Endurance level: Easy–Moderate

Tip: On the skinniest stretches of road, ride in the centre to discourage any idiotic passes from rare motor vehicles.

Contacts:
National Trails
www.nationaltrail.co.uk

The Ridgeway
www.ridgeway40.org.uk

LONDON, ENGLAND

With its vast sprawling jigsaw of 'villages', famous Royal Parks, instantly recognisable iconic landmarks and fine historic monuments, London pieces together around the mighty curves of the River Thames and its many bridges. Commuters, sightseers and residents in this handsome capital city move around on foot, by tube (underground train) or in its famous red buses or black taxis. And, since 2010 they have also had a self-service bike-hire scheme dotted all over the capital, to help them get from A to B. Originally named 'Boris Bikes' after the former London Mayor Boris Johnson, himself a well-known cyclist, the scheme has more than 10,000 bikes at over 700 docking stations and offers a quick and easy alternative to stuffy tube carriages and pricey taxi rides. As Boris said, at the launch of this two-wheeled initiative, 'the best way to see London in all its glory is by bike'.

Seeing London from the saddle of a bike needn't involving risking life and limb on its chaotic streets because there are plenty of awesome back-routes that have risen to prominence in recent years. Perfect for short journeys, the hire bikes are a great way to travel to a meeting, pop to the shops, meet friends or take in the fantastic sights of London. No membership is required: you can just hire a bike with your credit or debit card, ride it where you like and return it to any docking station: there is one every 330–550 yards (300–500 metres), but if you're uncertain where to find them, Transport for London's website has a map and list of them all. The bikes are available for rent 24 hours a day, 365 days a year. Due to the success of the scheme, bikes are now available anywhere from Canary Wharf to Camden Town and from Wandsworth to the Westfield in Shepherd's Bush.

The bike access fee for the day costs £2 and includes the first 30 minutes. After that, it's another £2 for every 30 minutes or less. There's no limit to how many trips you can take in a day and you only have to wait five minutes between docking a bike and taking out another one. If you damage or don't return a bike, you could face a fine of up to £300. You have to be over fourteen to ride one of the bikes.

Although it is less than ten years since the bikes were introduced to England's capital, it is hard to remember a time London was without them. Many Londoners still spend much of their time journeying their beautiful city underground and so rarely get to see its lush parks or towering spires. However, a growing number of people have made a scoot on these hire bikes part of their commute in the capital. Visitors, too, seem smitten by the quirks of the bikes and how they have opened up London's parks, back alleys and lesser known routes.

For a two-hour trip out from Greenwich to Blackheath, pick up your bike at South Quay in ultra-modern Canary Wharf, then cycle along the picturesque waterside routes of Docklands down to the Isle of Dogs in the east of the city, famously bounded on three sides by one of the largest meanders in the River Thames. Then keep going in a straight line and dismount for the foot tunnel that will take you under the Thames and on to the south side at Greenwich. After marvelling at the *Cutty Sark*, the world's sole surviving tea clipper and fastest ship of her time, it's time to cycle up through magnificent Greenwich Park, one of London's famous Royal Parks accessed via Blackheath Avenue, The Avenue or Great Cross Avenue. Every year millions of Londoners and tourists visit Greenwich Park, one of eight leafy Royal Parks in London. Greenwich Park hosts the Prime Meridian Line and Royal Observatory and is part of the Greenwich Maritime World Heritage Site that is home to the National Maritime Museum and Old Royal Naval College. The most historic of all Royal Parks, Greenwich Park dates back to Roman times and was enclosed in 1433. From the statue of General Wolfe, the park offers imperious views across the River Thames all the way to St Paul's Cathedral.

The Royal Parks provide fantastic 'green' routes in London, taking cyclists away from traffic and through some of its most attractive areas. Cycling is allowed on all roads and some specially designated cycle routes within the Parks – the only exception is Primrose Hill. Many of the routes link in with the wider London Cycle Network. Greenwich Park is an outstanding place to visit. As well as being of major historic importance and a World Heritage Site, the Park is also a Grade I listed landscape and a Site of Metropolitan Importance for Nature Conservation as the home to London's bats, birds, rare wildflowers and grasses – in short, a real haven for wildlife. Originally, they wandered around the whole area, but over time the deer were moved away from the more popular sections of the Park until they were confined to The Wilderness, by the Flower Garden in the south-east. There are paths leading to special viewpoints from which you can enjoy watching the herd of sixteen fallow deer and fourteen red deer.

The secluded woodland and ancient trees in The Wilderness also provide a sanctuary for other wildlife. Standing and lying dead wood is left to decay naturally, providing an important habitat for various invertebrates, especially beetles such as the stag beetle. Stag beetles develop as larvae in decaying stumps for up to seven years before emerging as adults. Such undisturbed areas are therefore vitally important, and also provide a refuge for birds, bats,

Photo: Bjørn Erik Pedersen

foxes, wood mice and many other animals. The ancient trees and dead wood are also important for fungi.

In 2002 the Secret Garden Wildlife Centre was created from a derelict building with the support of the Friends of Greenwich Park. The Centre includes educational equipment and information regarding flora and fauna, a small classroom, kitchenette and toilets. The classroom is also a hide with one-way glass in the windows so deer and wildlife can be observed without the animals being aware. Back on the road, head past the planetarium and keep going straight until you eventually reach Blackheath, a sprawling 85 hectares (21 acres) of protected commons with a fascinating history as the birthplace of golf, the scene of an ancient peasant revolt and a medieval burial pit during the Black Death. Cycle down towards the church, then the railway station and you'll find the Railway Inn on the right. This old pub serves decent traditional British grub, such as fish and chips and roast beef, and pours a really good pint of British draft beer. Grab a seat, rest up and absorb the pub atmosphere – you'll deserve it after 120 minutes on a two-wheeled 'Boris'.

Endurance level: Easy–Moderate

Tip: Second hand, well-thumbed guide books should be easy to come across in backpacker hostels and budget traveller cafes – cycle maps too.

Contacts:
Transport for London
www.tfl.gov.uk/modes/cycling/santander-cycles

EUROPE

SIERRA NEVADA, SPAIN

After a couple of days of blissful cycling in warm Spanish sunshine, things are about to get significantly more serious. Gradient signs in red are further emphasised by over-sized exclamation marks. My map looks alarming too: a spaghetti of tangled contour lines and elevations in a scary mix of colours. I gingerly approach the foothills of the Sierra Nevada and gradually allow myself to study the slopes beyond me. Dios mío! A slow-burning pain in my calves is fully registering on my radar and somehow it feels fitting that I should curse in the local lingo.

Like a puff of cloud, I've breezed along for an entire weekend feeling more than a little smug at the ease with which I progress. Now, however, I am developing a pathological hatred for my saddle, once relatively comfy but now an instrument of torture. I am also suffering from rather peculiar hazy hallucinations, no doubt prompted by the altitude. After navigating a succession of Volvo-sized potholes, I'm seriously tempted to sell my soul for just a few metres of asphalt. The Sierra Nevada's legendary debilitating fatigue is already kicking in and bits of me are purple, red and blue: bruised, raw and saddle sore.

Give up? Not a chance: these aching limbs are well worth the rewards of two-wheeling the highest peak in Spain. A picnic of chorizo, olives, bread and cheese helps to revive my

Photo: Jebulon

flagging spirits as I pedal on high into the Sierra Nevada, leaving the steamy 36°C humidity-laden summer behind in favour of the clouds.

Here it's a glorious 25°C, with no wind to speak of. There isn't much oxygen either at 3,000 metres (9,843 feet), so once the adrenaline-thrill of reaching the top subsides, an overwhelming sense of fatigue kicks in. Altitude can also play havoc with your emotions, coordination and judgement, so it's best not to make any big life-changing decisions at the peak. Mentally, I make a note to avoid marriage proposals or honest calls to my boss, just in case my reasoning is skewed.

Like many other cyclists before me, I've limbered up on the valley slopes from the village of Capileira, the topmost settlement in the Poqueira Gorge. Picture-postcard wooden-beamed white-washed Alpujarran houses topple over narrow, winding streets. A road hemmed by varicoloured pot-plants climbs out of the village and looks out over rooftops dotted with pepper-pot chimneys to a stunning panorama. I contentedly pat the pedals to pass cactuses and lush, leafy vegetation before things toughen up and the road is swallowed up by piles of crumbling rocks.

Accommodation is offered by way of the Refugio del Poqueira, where I join a civilised bunch of hairy, bearded outdoor-types to overnight at 2,500 metres (8,202 feet). Over a sumptuous three-course meal of rabbit, complete with Andalusian wine, we swap tales of lunar-like dry river beds, forest trails and pea-soup fog, relishing every morsel.

Thanks to the scrambling hooves of mountain goats and a relay of contrabandistas, the Sierra Nevada boasts more well-formed single-track gully trails than they can shake an isotonic energy drink at – and all of it natural. Terrain ranges from sprouting farmland in the foothills through pine thickets to craggy barren peaks. Dry, dusty sinuous stretches dwindle to loosely scattered rocks in an instant with steep sandy ravines and nail-biting drops. Tangled roots and gnarled knotty creepers weave through skinny ferns and scrub on the unworldly trail up to Veleta – the second highest peak in Spain at 3,396 metres (11,142 feet) and a hellish climb along a chilly, windblown ridge where ledges of snow cling determinedly in sheltered crevices, even in August. Deeper drifts can force an undignified dismounting on the more dishevelled snow-crusted flanks, making it easier pride-wise to get off and walk. Then it's a steady slog up through jagged, rock-scattered mayhem to Pico Veleta, where jaw-dropping views produce an involuntary intake of breath – all of it bug-free. It is here that I realise that my body has finally got used to the jolts and jars in the saddle, or has given up protesting about it. I imbibe the fragrance of damp mist and forest, gulp down several bottles of water and drink in the all-consuming quiet.

Next, it's an epic three-in-one vertical descent at eye-popping velocity through the wilderness to Orgiva – not something for anyone who is gravity-shy. Picking a line between the rocks requires brow-furrowing concentration as I hurtle through nineteen kilometres (twelve miles) of desert – an exhilarating, downhill thrill at speeds of 40 kilometres per hour (25 miles per hour). The Sierra Nevada springs to life in the summer as wild flowers and herbs sprout up, spreading a colourful blanket and filling the air with scent. Tiny white-washed weather-beaten villages hug the mountainsides, while vultures and eagles swoop and soar in the thermals overhead.

Endurance level: Difficult

Tip: Save some stamina for the final leg – the climb is fearsome.

Contacts:
Biking Andalusia
www.bikingandalucia.com

Andalucia Tourist Board
www.andalucia.org

Spanish Tourist Board
www.tourspain.es

ANGOULÊME, FRANCE

A line drawn around the route of the Circuit des Remparts in the historic walled city of Angoulême forms an enticing squiggle packed with tight curves and wriggly switchback bends, linking the Cathedral St Pierre to the turn at Jerome Tharaud. This world-renowned classic car street race takes place on the third weekend in September each year, on a crowded circuit. Located about 45 minutes from Cognac, in the heart of the Charente district, Angoulême's atmospheric ancient core – the Cité des Valois – is encircled by imposing ramparts and a riddle of climbing, narrow roads. On race day, amidst a flurry of brightly coloured flags and bunting, the historic quarter closes off to form a highly demanding street circuit. Highly polished classic cars gleam in anticipation at the start-line, from the Bugatti, Riley and MG racers of the pre-war category to post-war Porsche 911s and TVRs. Angoulême's fearsome combination of hairpin bends and lightning-fast straights requires spine-tingling driving precision. Cars roar past crowds of spectators just a few inches from grand medieval buildings that provide a spectacular throwback to bygone years. Handsome solid stone walls do much to enhance the drama as the resonating blasts of vintage exhausts hail the start of one of the most perilous races on the planet.

On a bike, even a brand new alloy model, I'm unlikely to clock up eye-popping speeds on the per-lap distance of 1.279 kilometres (0.795 miles). However, I will get to feel the gravity of the right-angle bends and tight twists and turns of this extraordinary race course. As a competitive cycle sprint route, guided by ramparts of the city, it is an easy to navigate fast-paced dash that takes some beating. Almost two-thirds of the route runs atop the city to offer striking views of the scenery beyond, while the statuesque cathedral provides an imposing start/finishing line. As a motor sports route, the Angoulême International Circuit des Remparts is the only inner city racing circuit whose layout has remained unchanged since it was created in 1939.

To achieve a decent time as I race around Angoulême's tight, switchback bends, I revisit some of the fundamentals of my basic cycling technique. On a route like this, the pedalling, gearing and braking need to be so smooth and fluid as to be imperceptible. My hips should be still, my cadence steady and I should feel at one with my bike. The thing about bike-handling is that it requires plenty of practice to master it. In my head I will myself to be more like Bradley Wiggins, with his effortless glide and oh-so-seamless cornering. To ride the Circuit des Remparts route well is to ride with cool, calm confidence, otherwise I risk leaving a lot of skin on the road. In readiness, I get on the drops with my fingers on the brakes to maximise traction and control. I also level myself out on the saddle to ensure the distribution of my body weight is even between the front and rear tyres. I

Photo: JLPC

wobble, alarmingly, so resolve to go steady. I shift my weight to the outside leg so I can cut a tighter line. Uneven road surfaces and bumps, potholes and traffic are all hazards on the route and I am poised to keep an eagle eye out for manhole covers and road markings. One of my worst traits is braking too hard, which on this route could cause my bike to skid. There are few opportunities to straighten out a corner along the track in Angoulême, so I will need to slow right down before the death-defying turn on the lung-busting homeward stretch.

On the day I'm in Angoulême, I'm joined on the circuit by a time trial veteran from Canada and a Spaniard on a racing trike. Cyclists often visit Angoulême's Circuit des Remparts as they pass through Charente while on the EuroVelo network (otherwise known as the Pilgrims Route). Created from fourteen cycling routes that stretch across Europe, the 5,122-kilometre (8,182-mile) Pilgrims Route connects Trondheim in Norway to Saint Jacques de Compostela in Spain. The Canadian, Spaniard and I decide to attempt the Circuit des Remparts together and I'm grateful for the companionship along a particularly challenging series of frightening dog-legs that scale the ramparts on a gradient. We reach a tearing pace towards an imaginary black-and-white-chequered flag. It may be a far cry from lap speeds of 70 kilometres per hour (43.5 miles per hour) achieved by the likes of Porsche and Bugatti, but it is still deserving of the traditional Angoulême winner's lap of honour – which we deliver, the two wheeled way.

Endurance level: Moderate

Tip: Wear bright clothes along this bendy route – visibility is all-important on the blind switchbacks.

Contacts:
Circuit International des Remparts d'Angoulême
www.circuit-des-remparts.com

Charente Tourist Board
www.visit-poitou-charentes.com

ROUTE DES VINS, FRANCE

The scenery may be postcard picturesque, but don't let the genteel charm of the Route des Vins deceive you: discovering Alsace on two-wheels requires a slog along a long and wineding road. Top-notch athletes with a fervent enthusiasm for the saddle will find the gentle, sloping stretches a breeze. Yet, in the unrelenting searing summer heat, the route's shadeless climbs are a gruelling test of endurance. Thankfully, a scattering of rustic stone water-fountains offer panting cyclists much-needed irrigation. Few things are as thrilling as free-wheeling downhill at speed just a stone's throw from Germany and the Rhine, past 119 half-timbered villages in a rainbow of bubble-gum hues.

Although it's possible to cycle from Strasbourg itself, the city's traffic-heavy streets and suburbs are worth giving a miss. Instead, head to the pretty stone villages around handsome Blienschwiller about 39 kilometres (24 miles) to the north-west. The entire Wine Route stretches some 170 kilometres (106 miles) from Gimbrett in the north to Leimbach in the south, a stretch doable in a long weekend. A shorter burst from Blienschwiller to Riquewihr is about a 60-kilometre (37-mile) round trip – hardly the Tour de France, admittedly,

Photo: Maximilian Dörrbecker

but almost all of it congestion-free. Yet with the blue-green Vosges Mountains and the crags of the Black Forest as distractions – not to mention 7,000 winegrowers and 14,500 hectares (35,830 acres) of vines – choosing to do a more intense, cherry-picked snapshot of the Route des Vins is an excellent option for those up against the clock.

More than 8 million visitors make the pilgrimage to the Wine Route each year, not all of them by bike. Those who do, however, will experience some of France's most stunning countryside along with plenty of challenges to conquer. Most tour companies deliver bikes to your door, spokes and sprockets checked and tyres fully pumped. Then, simply unfurl a map to gauge the physical demands ahead: the spaghetti riddle of wiggly lines is testament to an upcoming series of hills. An initial easy stretch through Dambach-la-Ville, Dieffenthal, Scherwiller, Kintzheim and Châtenois eases cyclists into the saddle, but is merely a light appetiser for a meatier entrée. Yellow-green vines and red-roofed cottages form a checkerboard landscape, dotted with Gothic spires and turrets. Forests, ramparts and ancient ruins are surrounded by meadows of sweet-smelling wildflowers. It is impossible not to become lost in the rush of scenery as the kilometres whiz by, such is the heady freedom of Alsace's vine-hemmed open roads. Rorschwihr, a small hamlet, lays down the first gauntlet. It's a skyward climb, prompting a gripping of handlebars, lowering of head and gritting of teeth as the pedals are pounded with vigour. Rows of proud saluting vines greet the sweat-beaded triumphant. In summer, a field of beaming, weathered farm-workers are also prone to imparting words of advice on the quirks of the road ahead.

Freewheeling through Kintzheim and Orschwiller and out towards Saint-Hippolyte allows a chance for the adrenaline to surge as the speedometer hits the max. Towards Rorschwihr the road widens and becomes busier as farm trucks and tractors chug past followed by a stream of slow-moving cars. One hilly kilometre leads to another, yet the constant visual stimulation of the magnificent Wine Route's vine-clad contours helps dull the pain of tiring limbs. Another source of motivation is the super-fit professional road-racing cyclists who favour the route, whooshing by effortlessly, legs waxed and oiled. Competitive types will find that just the sight of such an über human can trigger an incredible surge in natural power, sparking an energetic out-of-the-saddle sprint in pursuit of a moving cloud of dust on the horizon.

From Rorschwihr, where the route edges out towards Bergheim, a leaf-shrouded water-pump dispenses an ice-cold gin-clear dousing. The barrel-fronted Gilbert Dontenville winery signifies that Ribeauville is just a few kilometres away, along an immaculate tarmac carpet. Only the seriously virtuous will be able to resist the lure of slithers of scrumptious Tarte Flambé served at the roadside. Negotiating Ribeauville isn't half as troublesome as it looks on the map: simply skirt the edge of the town, loop a couple of mini-roundabouts and follow the road to Riquewihr. Free again from the urban melee, the route becomes distinctly bucolic with a light scattering of simple farm buildings on rounded yellow meadows. The long climb to Hunawihr and Riquewihr weaves past bougainvillea-filled barrels and swaying wrought iron signs temptingly shaped like wine bottles. Stamina and staying power are essential for this final leg, so be sure to have a croissant stashed in a pannier somewhere to help muster much-needed reserves. The ornate archways and fairy-tale world of Riquewihr provide a strangely magical finale, complete with castles, jutting Rapunzel-style towers and Cinderella spires. A mammoth novelty wineglass (well, we are on the Route des Vins) provides a good place to tether bikes while you sample a vintage. Seek out a crisp sparking Crément at the Au Cep de Vigne to toast tired joints to the sweet-smelling aroma of cinnamon biscuits and strains of Bavarian oom-pah classics.

Endurance level: Moderate

Tip: Invest in extra-large panniers for this trip – you're certain to be tempted by bottles of local wine sold by the roadside.

Contacts:
Tourism-Alsace
www.tourisme-alsace.com

Alsace Route des Vins
www.alsace-wine-route.com

FLANDERS BATTLEFIELDS, BELGIUM

The outbreak of the First World War, which pitted Germany, Austria-Hungary and the Ottoman Empire (the so-called Central Powers) against Great Britain, France, Russia, Italy and Japan (the Allied Powers), saw unprecedented levels of carnage and destruction. Gruelling trench warfare and the introduction of modern weaponry such as machine guns, tanks and chemical weapons took warring to another level. By the time the First World War ended in November 1918 more than 9 million soldiers had been killed and 21 million more wounded. Today, the battlefields of 'The Great War', as it was known, provide a poignant reminder of the price of conflict on such a scale. In Flanders, around the extended Westhoek area, a fascinating network of cycling trails snake around the various battlefields, along rolling well-kept trails, to discover how the profound impressions of the Great War remain a legacy today.

With a level terrain, striking scenery and hundreds of well-signposted cycling routes, Flanders is a bike lover's dream. A nice mix of routes offers plenty that are suitable for beginners and families, while there are also longer pathways to ensure more challenging, full-day options. Exploring the battlefields of the First World War by bike combines compelling history and poignancy with bracing views. After a century of reflection, the places where such mammoth sacrifices occurred are still humbling to witness. Cycling between locations provides a unique opportunity to appreciate the landscape and geography.

Highlights include Messines Ridge, Tyne Cot Cemetery, Hill 60, Fromelles, Vimy Ridge, Pals battalions memorials, Newfoundland Memorial Park, the Thiepval memorial to the Missing of the Somme and the site of the Christmas Truce football match of 1914. A number of specialist tour operators offer tailored itineraries to cyclists (solo, small groups or larger tours) to reflect personal connections to Flanders, the soldiers of a particular nation and places of global significance. Most tours start with attending the Last Post ceremony at the Menin Gate – a tribute to the dead and missing of the Ypres Salient that has been enacted every day since 1928 except during the German occupation (and then it was re-instigated even as the Germans were retreating from the other end of the town in 1944). The Menin Gate bears the names of some 55,000 soldiers with no known grave. In

Photo: Wernerve

fact, it was not large enough to inscribe all the names of the missing and another 35,000 were recorded at Tyne Cot, one of the largest cemeteries of the First World War. In addition to these names are 12,000 graves – a sobering place to visit. If you're cycling independently, be sure to pick up a copy of *The Great War in Flanders 1914–1918 Battle Map* as it covers all of the key sites with exceptional detail and highlights the locations of the various First World War memorial sites, annotated by nationality and/or colour-coded for different stages of the war, and cross-referenced to a 64-page multilingual guide. It combines the clearest road map and the largest numbers of marked sites over a base map that shows the present-day road network. Indispensable. Even if you're travelling with a tour group, I'd recommend taking this with you.

Other stopping points include the location where John McCrae wrote the poem 'In Flanders Fields', which eloquently established the poppy flower as the symbol of remembrance. Also the point where the Germans carried out the first gas attack in the second battle of Ypres in 1915 and the 44,000 graves of German soldiers at the Langemark cemetery. Quiet backroads lead to the historical military sites of Tyne Cot and Hill 60. There are more key points in the south, including the mine craters of the Messines Ridge, a tactically important point because it held the high ground on the southern arc of the Ypres Salient and diverted German troops from the Battle of Arras.

Riding through Gommecourt and Serre takes you to the places where huge sacrifices were made, including the largest single-day loss in the history of the British Army. The Newfoundland Memorial Park reminds visitors that the Newfoundland Regiment was all but wiped out: all of its officers and 90 per cent of its men were killed or wounded on 1 July 1916. Much of the pastoral scenery that you cycle through with its pretty stone walls, wildflowers and lush pasture, are areas that experienced bitter hand-to-hand fighting – a far cry from peaceful tranquillity today. An extremely good planning tool for any trip to First World War sites in Flanders is an online interactive map of battlefields at www.fietsroute.org.

Endurance level: Easy

Tip: Have plenty of bottled water to hand on this trip as it isn't widely sold along this route.

Contacts:
Flanders Fields
www.flandersfields.be/en

Belgium 1914–18
www.be14-18.be/en

The Great War
www.greatwar.co.uk

AMSTERDAM, NETHERLANDS

Rightly known as the 'City of Bikes', Amsterdam and cycling have a long association. More than 40 per cent of rush-hour traffic is in two-wheeled man-powered mode. Some 800,000 cycles weave, wobble, race and screech along Amsterdam's confusing maze of canal paths, cobblestone streets and over bridges. In Holland, bikes are not only practical, efficient, economic and environmentally friendly, they are positively endorsed as King of the Roads, especially when it comes to parking. In a nation of 16.4 million, bike ownership runs at more than 17 million with over 3.4 million choosing to do their daily commute in the saddle. In Amsterdam, cycle possession averages at 1.1 per person with function overwhelmingly valued over style. Battered old rust-covered bone-shakers outnumber the city's sleek, stream-lined gleaming machines. Amsterdam's beloved bike, the single-gear Oma, boasts solid handlebars, thick tires and a pair of industrial-sized locks, one for the frame and one for the back wheel. Rules of the road appear forgotten by riders young and old. Speed also is compulsory, especially when the distinctive clanging of a tram bell tolls.

Every hotel and B&B in Amsterdam offers bike hire and tours. Rental booths can be found in train stations across the city, while Damstraat, Holland Rent-a-Bike and MacBike do a roaring trade. Expect to pay about 20 Euros a week (or 5–8 Euros a day) for Amsterdam's trademark black municipal model. Grab a bike-path map (Amsterdam op de fiets, meaning 'Amsterdam on the Bike', 4 Euros) from the VVV tourist information office outside Central Station for a standard urban meander. Some specially crafted alternatives have been created by Amsterdam's Infrastructure, Traffic and Transportation department (dienst Infrastuctuur, Verkeer en Vervoer) in collaboration with Amsterdam's Cyclists' Union (Fietsersbond) to mark the occasion of the Vélo Mondial 2000. However, for the ultimate thrill off the metropolis's beaten track, ask the guys at MacBike for a few hot tips – but be sure use to a lightweight, high-velocity machine.

Navigating Amsterdam's 400-kilometre (249-mile) muddle of cycle paths (*fietspaden*) is confused by Holland's perplexing right-of-way rules, a theoretical framework that, in practice, is open to loose interpretation. According to the rulebook, traffic coming from your left should give you the right of way, but it pays to err on the side of caution. Each of Amsterdam's cycle paths is lavished with an amount of care and attention usually reserved for Royal visits. Regular caretaking schedules involve sprucing-up, power-washing, de-icing, sweeping and debris clearance. A round blue sign with a white bicycle indicates a dedicated bike lane – although, rather bafflingly, mosquito-engined mopeds are allowed to use the route too. City maps denote areas closed to cyclists, bike repair shops and flat tyre specialists, en route from Amsterdam's northern islands to the leafy suburbs in the south.

As a city poorly equipped for cars, Amsterdam's 17th-century narrow streets and skinny canal paths make a good place to hit the road. The city is flat and compact, with a maximum distance across the centre of around seven kilometres (four miles), an ideal distance to settle into the saddle. All manner of cycle-friendly initiatives make bike travel a breeze, from umpteen bike parking facilities and Amsterdam's positive cycle culture to the inauguration of a 'green wave' on the Raadhuisstraat, where cyclists travelling at a constant speed of around 15–18 kilometres per hour (nine to eleven miles per hour) catch every green light, thanks to a synchronised timing system. Amsterdam's frenzied flow of traffic even has its very own expert bicycle co-ordinator to manage the day-to-day needs of cyclists, including those with a desire to race along urban back-routes. Even off-beat inner-city routes on an industrial landscape include breezy rural sections that whiz past dykes and historical land reclamation sites.

One of Amsterdam's most adventurous urban cycle routes starts at the Haarlemmerplein by the 1840 triumphal arch with clock, Willemspoort. Zoom under the six-track rail

Photo: MARELBU

viaduct, past Planciusstraat's industrial lifting bridges, to the speed-gathering Houtmanstraat, a string of reclaimed 19th-century social housing. Cross bridges straddling barge-strewn canals in the Zoutkeetsgracht, to the old quayside of Houtmankade and the frenetic pace of traffic on busy van Diemenstraat. Fly by West Amsterdam's prime canal shipment passage, lurch along chaotic Tasmanstraat, past dykes, timber docks and re-excavation projects and slums scheduled for gentrification. Pump the pedals along the history-packed sea dyke route towards Haarlem past fuel stations, geriatric warehouses and fine old ports. Nip along two-way cycle paths on the Nieuwe Hemweg to race past railway tracks, freight depots, cooling towers, motorway viaducts and the North Sea Canal.

Push on past oil tanks, grain terminals, coal shipment depots and recycling plants before bumping down the path towards the former national Artillery Establishment (Staatsbedrijf der Artillerie-Inrichtingen). Board ferries, traverse one of Holland's original first-generation traffic routes and whiz around Zaandam and Westzaan. Pass medieval sea dykes, coffee-coloured estuaries, stepped alleys, pumping stations, farm buildings, open pasture, Jewish cemeteries and green-painted weatherboard houses. See old locks, container warehouses and towering cranes and also 18th-century windmills and churches steeped in aged splendour. Race aside old peat-powered paper mills, motorway embankments, reed-covered marshlands and lowland scrub to follow the sickly-sweet aroma of local cocoa factories. Cycle along riverside boardwalks and riverbank trails, past factory buildings, lock-houses and a shrine to Peter the Great.

The road back into Amsterdam city centre allows a chance to weave in and out of the urban melee towards Zaanstraat.

Sprint along a rat-run cycle path under a railway bridge before making a triumphant return into Haarlemmerplein at speed – just remember to pedal backwards to brake to a halt, a quirk of the Dutch cycle.

Endurance level: Easy–Moderate

Tip: On busier stretches leave ample space between your bike and the curb – you may need to pull in when trucks cut in close.

Contacts:
Amsterdam Tourist Office
www.iamsterdam.com

Rent a Bike
RentaBike.nl

Dutch Cycle Union (KNWU)
www.knwu.nl

SOUTH FYN ARCHIPELAGO, DENMARK

Even an enchanting land of fairy-tale make-believe has its monsters, but in Denmark's Hans Christian Andersen country the demons are a composition of nature. Among the magical fields of flowers, castles and windmills of Fyn (Funen) that provided inspiration for storyteller's tales of fairies and princesses lie some fiendish unpaved cycle tracks. Criss-crossing manicured asphalt roads, these rugged tyre-worn trails lead across the hop-filled meadows of the South Fyn Archipelago. Cycling through this picture-book area is to journey past legend-steeped and moat-ringed towers and spires. Denmark's circular 'Garden Island' sits in the centre of the country, forming a convenient 2,985-square-kilometre (1,855-square-mile) stepping-stone in the channel between Jutland and Zealand.

As befitting a 'cycle-friendly' nation, the Danish government publishes a map of its several-hundred cycle routes, over 100 of which run through Fyn. Published by the Danish Cycling Association, the *Cykleguide* is available from tourist offices nation-wide. Millions of Danes cycle every day and the nation is fully geared-up for cyclists of all types. Dozens of cycle hire companies, bike repair shops, tour guides and cycling package holidays address the needs of holidaying cyclists in Denmark with the Fyn area top of their list.

There are cycle paths in every city in Denmark – that's well over 12,000 kilometres (7,457 miles) of sign-posted cycle routes. New towns are planned with cycle paths in mind to make full use of the gentle terrain, inspirational nature and short distances between amenities. You'll see signs proclaiming 'We LOVE bikes!' all over Denmark and with smooth, asphalt trails that are perfectly maintained cycling is safe for families, not too strenuous and great fun. Download routes maps from the Danish Tourist Board website or pick up a local guide from the many tourist information points nation-wide. Each path has a route name, number and a distinctive logo that makes a trail easy to follow. Routes criss-cross each other, so it is simple to tailor your ride. And with cycle-paths running along small byroads, forest trails and country trails, you can explore the entire country by bike. National routes are signposted with a white route number in a red square and a bicycle symbol on a blue, square sign. Regional and local cycle routes have their own individual signage: regional routes are numbered 16 to 99 and local routes 100 to 999.

A popular 55-kilometre (34-mile) route connects the tiny market town of Bogense with Odense via the beaches of Hasmark Strand and offers a mix of paved and unmade tracks on a full-day's ride. As Denmark's second-largest island, Fyn is nourished by a year-round maritime climate. So it's wet in winter, dry in summer and sea-sprayed in between. Narrow roads weave through fishing villages of half-timbered houses still home to sea-legged mariners poised for combat with sand eel, herring and cod. Numerous interconnecting cycle paths and narrow winding roads exploit the easy views of this magnificent, idyllic and varied Danish countryside and offer a chance to sightsee at a comfortable pace, with the sea never far away. In spring and summer, the abundance of country flora bombards the senses with bright colours and fragrances.

Nature has bestowed Fyn with a rich variety of plants, shrubs, herbs, flowers and trees and around every languid bend in the road there is another jaw-dropping floral display. Giant mansions bear witness to the prosperity of ages past, while simple timber smallholdings, tucked in among the gentle hills, are surrounded by cultivated fields. Sweet-scented lilac draped across bird-filled hedgerows enhances the dazzling yellow of the fields of rape and corn. With no insurmountable climbs, the highest point on Fyn is Frøbjerg Bavnehøj at just 131 metres (430 feet) high and can be enjoyed by child and adult cyclists as part of an active family holiday. Hotels, holiday houses, campsites and youth hostels all cater for cyclists and provide a luggage transport service for holiday-makers keen to keep their rides hassle-free. Without the burden of luggage, it is easier to park up and

Photo: Peter Larsen

head off to explore the countryside on foot or to incorporate museum visits, sailing trips and guided tours. The sailing trips themselves also constitute a delightful interlude, as the routes between the islands are plied not only by actual ferries, but also tour boats and authentic wooden sailing ships – a magical glimpse into Danish maritime history.

Cyclists keen for adventure without excessive fatigue will enjoy Fyn's gently undulating countryside. Only a couple of intimidating hills invoke any huffing and puffing with off-road trails providing exhilaration in short, manageable bursts. Views of this fabled terrain are best absorbed along the hidden back-roads, passing shimmering lakes, dragon-flies, windmills and jumping fish. From the medieval gatehouses of Gyldensten, a tougher road leads to the woodlands of Sandagergård Manor. It then winds down to the unspoiled shores and dykes of Hasmark Strand – the perfect spot for a cooling dip.

Odense Fjord is an important resting place for Denmark's migratory bird species and a breeding ground for gulls, terns, herons and swans. Nip across expanses of moorland vegetation, such as juniper, heather and crowberry, watching out for adders, grass snakes and sand lizards. Race parallel with a narrow strip of pebble beach bordered by salt plains and reed swamps close to tumbledown cottages in vibrant Barbie-pink hues.

Endurance level: Easy

Tip: Watch the roads after heavy rain showers when smooth, shiny surfaces can be as slippery as ice.

Contacts:
VisitDenmark

www.visitdenmark.co.uk

VisitFyn
www.visitfyn.com

Cyclistic
www.cyclistic.dk/en

LOFOTEN ARCHIPELAGO, NORWAY

The Lofoten Archipelago hangs off the end of Norway's
north-western coast and is home to traditional fishing villages,
puffins and seals. Bucolic beauty and peaceful, open views
typify the laid-back character of the islands, where cyclists
flock to get their fix of 'off the radar' chill time. A delicate
scattering of small communities wait to be discovered along
quiet asphalted trails. As the home of hundreds of sea birds,
including the majestic sea eagle, which can be seen soaring
skilfully over the cliff-tops all year round, Lofoten is an avian
Shangri-La. Trail sections and distances are relatively short,
with the furthest ride, from Fiskebøl to Å along the E10,
around 160 kilometres (100 miles). Though every cycling
guide recommends waterproof and windproof clothing,
gloves, reflective vests, helmets, good lights and reflectors,
and a first-aid kit, in truth rides across Lofoten are generally
dry – unless sea spray drifts inland. Despite the fact that the
beaches of Lofoten lie on the wrong side of the Arctic Circle –
on the same latitude as you'll find polar bears – the brightest
summers see the mild climate achieve temperatures of 20°C
thanks to the warm Gulf Stream.

Photo: Zairon

Lofoten is perfect for outdoorsy fun: most of the cycling routes steer clear of the hills, ensuring they are ideal for families. Throw a fishing line from the jetty or enjoy a barefoot stroll across long, surf-swept sands. Join a guided sea-kayaking tour to explore hidden coves and islets. Speedy, high-powered RIBs (rigid inflatable boats) offer whistle-stop trips to narrower fjords as well as trips to watch white-tailed sea eagles. Full-day boat tours do battle with tumultuous seas to offer visitors a chance to see sperm whales in summer (and, in winter, humpback, fin and killer whales too). The summer months (late May to mid-July) also provide a magical opportunity to ride until the wee small hours under the eternal brightness of the midnight sun. What's more, the Northern Lights can be viewed here from September to mid-April.

Plenty of guided cycle trips and bike rental outlets are available, as well as multi-day tour packages that include accommodation, bicycle hire and cycling excursions as part of the deal. Alternatively, you can catch the cycle ferry and sort out your own route and B&B – detailed maps can be picked up from the transit terminal at Svolvær, the archipelago's capital and the point of arrival for those coming by air or sea. Booklets are also freely available at hotels, restaurants and other tourist points archipelago-wide and there are now English versions of the best-selling handbook *Hjulgleder*, which is an indispensable guide to exploring the islands by bike.

Maps helpfully detail hiking, skiing, fishing, ocean rafting, surfing (it is the world's most northernmost surfing hotspot and Norway's finest) and scuba diving in relation to all of the main cycle routes. Not a destination to sprawl lizard-like on a sweltering beach, these are islands to enjoy activity: from bracing walks, shoreline strolls and cycle rides across the islands to settling down with an easel and paints to capture the majesty of the scenery on canvas. Lofoten also has a strong connection to the Viking Age, and you'll find lots of maps and guides at the Lofotr Viking Museum about archaeological discoveries, such as a Viking longhouse: the largest ever unearthed here is over 80 metres (262 feet). Signs around the archipelago point out Viking heritage along the way. Enormous, expansive landscapes are surprisingly easily accessible via a network of trekking trails that dip in and out along the coastline. Beautiful fine white sand is lapped by light blue waters and is backed by rolling pastures and dramatic peaks that are still capped with snow, even in June. Don't miss an opportunity to drink in the giddy views from the top of the 690-metre (2,265-foot) Fløya – the path rises steeply, over rocky ground, through trees and alongside trickling meltwater, but the heart-in-your-mouth slog is richly rewarded with incredible views that stretch all the way to mainland Norway.

Favourite rides include a 65-kilometre scenic blast, Fiskebøl–Laukvik–Svolvær, which skirts the outer edge of Austvågøya through one of the region's most stunningly beautiful areas. You'll pass gorgeous sandy beaches, velvety green-grass slopes, butterfly-scattered moorland, lakes of the brightest blue and the chalky-white cliffs of the fjord. The Henningsvær–Stamsund route is a similar distance. Follow the E10 past Lyngvær and cycle over Gimsøystraumen Bridge – prepare to be wowed by the sweeping views – and enjoy lunch in the sleepy splendour of Gimsøy, where there are umpteen beautiful beaches and very few cars. Then take the RV 815 along the scenic southern edge before turning off onto Valbergveien along a relatively quiet country road, and cycle on to wilderness outpost Stamsund, with its squawking seabird colonies and spectacular sands. For centuries, fishing has been at the heart of the communities of Lofeton: you can stay overnight in old fishermen's cabins, eat stockfish made from spawning cod and watch the boats haul their nets in at dawn. The islands' many artists have long exploited the rapidly changing local weather and magnificent light conditions to capture the magnificent marine landscapes and produce exquisite watercolours and sculptures on seashore themes. Dine on fine shellfish at rustic eateries in beautiful ports such as Nusfjord, Henningsvær and Kabelvåg (which dates back to the ninth century, making it the oldest village above the Arctic Circle) among net menders, fish baskets and drying cod.

Endurance level: Moderate

Tip: Strong headwinds on the most exposed coastal roads can make the going tough in poor weather – so nip inland for an easier ride.

Contacts:
Norway Tourist Board
www.visitnorway.com

Lofoten
www.lofoten.info

MÜNSTER, GERMANY

In Münster, Germany's 'Bicycle Capital', children are tutored in cycling from the age of three, such is the city's enthusiasm. A daily bicycle (*leezen*) commute involves a belldinging two-wheeled rush hour. Bikes outnumber residents by almost two to one, while Münster's extensive cycle-path network boasts a designed 4.5-kilometre Bicycle Promenade used by 1,200 cyclists an hour. Even the city's car-strewn one-way system has been adapted to accommodate two-way cycle traffic. In November, a six-day Cycle Race brings the city to a virtual standstill, as the Olympiahalle stadium heaves with lean, two-wheeled warriors of the road – inducing a state of excitement matched only by the city-wide fervour that erupted when the Giro d'Italia bike race sprinted into town.

Italy's most important cycle race paid a visit to Germany in 2002 as part of the PR machine to plug the Euro, calling at Belgium, Luxembourg and Strasbourg, before whizzing off to its native Turin in what was billed a single currency transaction. Münster was awarded the honour of hosting the first stage of the 85th Giro d'Italia in 2002, a fitting accolade for a city so slavishly devoted to two-wheeled pursuits. The cavalcade clocked up record speeds as it raced over the German border, cutting through central and lower Emsland across a ripple of hedge-ringed meadows. The Giro d'Italia circus whipped Münster into a frenzy to further forge its bond with cycling. Today, residents spend an average of 15.6 minutes a day on two wheels, with 40.5 per cent of all inner city journeys made by bicycle. What's more, Münster has since built a flourishing tourist trade on the back of its Giro d'Italia pedigree, encouraging visitors to follow the first stage of the route by bike.

Over 100,000 citizens use the 'Leeze' – the translation of the word 'bicycle' in Münster dialect – on a daily basis in the city. As well as the cycle paths and trails, there are special bicycle roads on which the cyclists set the pace and take precedence over cars. A number of bicycle stations in Münster offer secure parking for cycles – the largest of these,

Photo: Dietmar Rabich

with its 3,500 parking spaces, is at the main railway station. It's not just a bike park but also has a repair centre, rental shop and bicycle washing station (lots of suds, spray jets and polish). You can also pick up hire bikes from the Münster Arkaden bicycle station, where shopping bags, rainwear or bicycle helmets can also be safely stowed away in lockers.

Outside the city of Münster, in the heart of the parkland that is the Münsterland Cycling Region, the cycle infrastructure is also impressive, with an enviable selection of bicycle parks, rental points, a network of cycle rental shops and cycling routes spanning an epic 4,500 kilometres (2,796 miles). Choose from a wide range of themed routes and circuits to suit every level of ability. You can also stay overnight in an excellent selection of B&B (Bed & Bike) accommodation run by knowledgeable cycle nuts. A new addition to Münster's bike scene is a trust-based cycle share scheme. Bike Surf is an up-and-coming bike lending charity that offers bikes for free, and asks for a voluntary donation rather than a fixed rental price. Look for the advertising hoardings in town, or the promotional marketing throughout the city – you can't miss it: 'Two wheels good: Free wheels better!'

A particularly good map, available from the Münster tourist information office, details the 218-kilometre route (in reverse) from Münster to Groningen (Netherlands), a small slice of the race's total 3,334-kilometre slog, but a full, hard day in the saddle nonetheless. To date, hundreds of would-be pace-lines have followed in the footsteps of stage winner Mario Cipollini, pounding the pedals at incredible speeds in true pink jersey style. Another adaptable route combines four interconnecting circuits that provide a flexible start and finish through the open countryside of the Münsterland region. Interspersed with numerous attractions, none of which are far apart, the main attractions include Versailles-like gardens, Gothic buildings and well-preserved monuments erected for grandeur – all of which can be accessed on two wheels. Tracks and trails are mainly flat with most cyclist-only asphalt well away from the traffic on busier roads. The circular routes run mostly through leafy parks, meadows and pastureland and visit the finest palaces, castles and stately homes in the region for a cultural and historical experience to remember.

From Münster at 59 metres (194 feet) the route to Groningen slopes to a five-metre elevation and is very much a sprinter's romp. For a nippy route closer to the city, speed off around the inner network of cycle paths, meshed together in honeycomb fashion to allow cyclists to tailor their own trips. Münster's Tourist Information Points also offer cycling tourists pocket PCs with satellite navigation to help direct them to the most fearsome hill-climbs and pinpoint decent recovery spots.

Endurance level: Moderate

Tip: This region is home to Germany's largest underground bicycle park, with 3,500 parking spaces!

Contacts:
Bike Surf Münster
www.BikeSurf.org/muenster

Münster Tourist Office
www.muenster.de

GURTEN, SWITZERLAND

Few days on a mountain bike are as perfect as those challenging long, scenic, downhill stretches with rocks, scary ledges, overhangs and jump-offs – without the nuisance of uphill slogs. Switzerland, a mountain-bike idyll with its rough terrain and perilous outcrops, requires bags of energy off-piste while rattling, loose-stone mountain trails demand maximum skill and control.

Although townies have tried their best to commandeer mountain biking, it is the world's most foreboding, jagged rocky ridges that play host to it in its purest form. 'The higher the better' has long been the mantra of a hard-core mountain bike crowd, who relish fearsome downhill runs against the odds. Crisscrossing tracks lead to full-tilt plunges across ravines in elevated airborne jumps. Roughly hewn trails carved from the rocks by the elements demand robust durability. Wide, knobby tyres, top-notch shock absorption and a sturdy frame make mountain bike models the weightiest in the cycle-world, with every bell and whistle on a downhill bike heavy duty – even a standard model tops in at around fifteen kilograms (33 pounds), despite continued efforts to shave off excess mass. Yet these powerful monsters of the mountains cope easily with unrelenting bumps, bashes and wipe-outs to withstand full-force impact on potholed back-roads, brutal single-tracks and trunk-strewn forested trails.

Swiss mountain bike routes are great for riders who enjoy remoteness and self-reliance, far from civilisation and where the risk of being stranded many kilometres from help is real. Long, full-day treks combine cross-country, downhill and free-riding – often with some street runs for good measure. Alpine shrub-covered razor-sharp crags, often spaced bike-length apart, provide the ultimate awkward hump and require a skilful pumping of the terrain. Rollers, small ditches, drops and debris from fallen branches demand precise, well-timed and confident negotiation. Bunny-hopping comes into its own when jumping and rattling over troublesome rocky ledges, while weight-fuelled racing-oriented downhill riding covers extremely steep terrain at terrifying speed, often using ski-runs in summer. Few rides are as physically demanding and dangerous for mountain bikers: they often include jumps of up to twelve metres (39 feet). Drops of three metres (ten feet) or more are a true test of commitment for even the most competent rider over an intimidating ragged jigsaw of razor-sharp peaks.

A particularly hair-raising trail is located in Bern's Wabern suburb and can be accessed by a 30-minute ride on the Gurtenbahn funicular train, ensuring no tiring uphill slog interferes with your downhill kicks. Buy a day card (around 20CHF) for the Gurten Park railway and allow 40CHF for the bike – special compartments are designated for storage. At the terminus at the top of the peak, the trail head is located about 50 metres (164 feet) down a paved path. A series of braking bumps lead to a short drop into the woods, where steeply banked sections offer a wide variety of jumps, allowing a great opportunity to boost technical moves. Don't take things too fast because some of the key features are obscured by the bigger lifts. Flatter routes trim the most complex trails, where riders of championship level will be tempted by a vast jump over a road gap – look out for a warning sign on the right-hand side.

Gurten is a favourite Bernese getaway and signature mountain, towering 280 metres (918 feet) above the city

Photo: Norbert Aepli, Switzerland

and 864 metres (2,835 feet) above sea level. As the closest mountain bike trail to the city centre, it can get crowded on Sundays but is open every day and is often totally isolated outside busier times. Ignore the touristy kids' play area and cafes to head to the wide expanse of countryside laced with tracks overlooking the city towards the Jura and across the peaks of the Bernese Oberland.

In Switzerland, you'll need a proper set of serious clothing for mountain biking, even on the most innocuous suburban trails. Temperatures plummet as soon as you reach a higher elevation and head protection is essential on rough, rocky mountainous trails. Gloves, protective eyewear, rough-terrain clothing and full body armour (including under jackets) are all advisable – you'll also need sunscreen, water bottles (or water bags) and a proper tool kit. In 2002 Bern proposed banning mountain biking on the region's single-track trails that were less than 1.2 metres (four feet) wide. Thankfully it was opposed by the Swiss cycling federation, foresters, law enforcement, tourism operators and grassroots bike advocacy organisations, who proved that bikers and hikers can share trails in respectful harmony. So Bern and its truly resplendent rugged terrain can still be enjoyed by a grateful international mountain bike crowd.

Mountain biking in nature is an essential part of the infrastructure for Swiss cycling athletes, including Switzerland's elite mountain bikers who ride the forest during training. Christoph Sauser, Nino Schurter, Florian Vogel, Thomas Litscher and Nathalie Schneitter are big names in the Bern cycling scene and regulars on single-track forest routes. Today, thousands of young riders, recreational mountain bike nuts and first-class sportspeople continue to enjoy the testing alpine thrills of the canton. Riders keen to join the crowds should arrive for the November Gurten

Classic, a mixed cycle race that includes a heavily subscribed 16.8-kilometre (ten-mile) mountain bike event.

Endurance level: Difficult

Tip: Invest in reflective strips on clothing, helmet and bike to improve your visibility with others on the road when it's misty and dull.

Contacts:
Bern Tourist Office
www.berninfo.com

Gurten – Park im Grünen
www.gurtenpark.ch

DANUBE RIVER PATH, AUSTRIA

With its pretty villages, enchanting gardens and mysterious rivers, cycling through Austria is like pedalling the pages of a fairy-tale book. Summertime scenery is particularly spectacular in rural Austria, and an enviable network of cycle lanes carry you through some truly delightful picture-perfect terrain. Although some Austrian roads are quite narrow, they are generally in perfect condition. Cycling is allowed everywhere, but if you want to leave other road users behind the bicycle-only pathways offer a ready escape. One of the most impressive cycle-ways follows the Danube River for 900 kilometres (559 miles) besides riverside dykes that hug canyons and peaks at the northern edge of the Alps.

Little wonder Austria's cycling community live by the mantra: 'Four wheels move the body. Two wheels move the soul'. This couldn't be truer than on this spirit-stirring route.

With an incredible choice of routes suiting riders of any ability, Austria offers every conceivable cycling holiday from extreme riding trails for cyclists keen to throw down a few tricks on a mountain bike trail to those who prefer to absorb the cultural views on a leisurely pedal. Austria champions cyclists at every turn and there is even a collection of 'Bed+Bike' accommodation along the Danube Cycle Path that is certified cycle-friendly. Not only do these B&Bs offer secure storage, bike 'first aid', e-charging, snacks, and hire bikes, a hearty breakfast is also assured in around 50 different locations between Vienna and Passau, including the Upper Austrian capital of Linz (a UNESCO City of Media Arts).

Running along Europe's second-longest river, once favoured by emperors and kings, this romantic cruising waterway meanders from Germany via Austria to Hungary. Cyclists have the benefit of not being limited to the course of the river: over 40 suggested cycling tours branch off the main path to delve into Austria's back country, both in the Upper Danube and Lower Danube regions of Austria out to where Vienna heads towards Budapest. For lovers of the e-bike, you'll be pleased to hear Austria has embraced this mode of cycling with gusto, installing charging stations and e-bike facilities along the Danube Cycle Path, together with a joined-up ticket that links e-bike riders to the public transport system. Find a copy of the Danube Cycle Path guide (available in second hand travel bookshops) for details of the suggested eleven stages (a tally of around 33 kilometres [twenty miles] each) complete with maps, route planners for additional cycle tours, details of e-bike rentals and charging stations – you can even download GPS data and print brochures as a PDF file: www.donauregion.at

No need to be a serious cyclist – the route is suitable for untrained riders and family cycle tours as well as experienced cyclists. To do it in a single stretch, the River Danube would probably take just over a week self-guided, moving from one hotel to another each day. A genteel, flat and scenic cycle path offers some sections you can do by train or boat – a boon if you're keen to spend a few hours out of the saddle. From Passau, head to Schlogen (43 kilometres/26 miles), then travel on to Upper Austria's media arts hub and the Capital of Culture in 2009, Linz. Straddling the Danube River midway between Salzburg and Vienna, Linz boasts some wonderful baroque buildings and a major modern art collection at the Kunstmuseum Linz (44 kilometres/28 miles plus train). Then it is the richly historic 4,000-year-old settlement of Enns at the mouth of the babbling Enns River (30 kilometres/eighteen miles) to Grein (43 kilometres/27 miles), the home of a fine flag-topped castle and the oldest theatre in Austria. Next the road weaves its way along the soft curves of the Wachau Valley to the small monastery town of Melk (48 kilometres/30 miles) before heading out to the brandy-making town of Krems (42 kilometres/26 miles) at the confluence of the Krems and Danube Rivers. After a week on-the-road, the final day in the saddle transports you to the regal opulence of the city of Vienna (44 kilometres/28 miles plus train) for a heady blur of gilded Hapsburg palaces, royal parks and magnificent Danube views.

Romance, tradition and charming Strauss waltzes still permeate through this magical city, from the dazzling chandelier-lit ballrooms, handsome buildings and the graceful white horses of the imperial stables to the cosy coffee houses, fine eateries, thrilling Ferris wheel and dark chocolate Sachertorte that beckon at every turn. Cruise the Danube

Photo: Willi Heidelbach

on a wine-tasting river boat, tour the city's backstreets in a genteel horse and carriage or soak up Vienna's joyous music scene in a wide variety of indoor and outdoor venues. The Viennese famously adore the captivating music of Wolfgang Amadeus Mozart and these musical symphonies can be enjoyed morning, noon or night in the city. Grab tickets for the opera house, a church performance, a festival, an open-air concert, or hear it at one of Vienna's glass-fronted Belle Epoque street cafes. The swirling rhythms and refrains of Mozart's musical creations will still be running through your mind as you explore the riverside bike trails around Vienna. A route map and guide are available at the Vienna Tourist Office, and you can rent sturdy city bikes at the ferry and train stations, or through all major Vienna hotels.

Endurance level: Easy–Moderate

Tip: Spirits flagging? This journey is fuel for the soul through breathtaking unspoiled countryside.

Contacts:
Danube Cycle Path
www.danube-cycle-path.com

Austria Tourist Board
www.austria.info

BRNO, CZECH REPUBLIC

Having long-tired of unfavourable comparisons with its prettier capital, the Czech Republic's oft-overlooked second city, Brno, has carved out a niche of its own. As a hub for cycling fanatics, Brno is the Czech Republic's bike-friendly city; a destination woven with cycle paths and trails. Sure, it may not have Prague's pastel-coloured aged architecture and handsome, picture-postcard streets, but Brno forms the very heart of the Czech Republic's sporting country. It is bounded by the striking Bohemian massif and leafy lowlands of Southern Moravia, with the Rivers Svratka and Svitava as a frame. Unlike Prague, Brno is less crowded over the summer months – the neon-lit nightlife shuts up shop once the students leave for the holidays (June to September), but everything else stays open and there's a nice, chilled-out vibe. So Brno will never be the new Prague, but the city shrugs its shoulders in the comfortable assurance that it has its own special gritty charm in amongst the tree-clad sloping hills.

Cyclists keen to get acquainted with Brno should check out the city's cracking 60-kilometre round-route to Pernštejn, one of the finest preserved Gothic fort-towns on the planet. A favourite ride with Brno cycling fans racing into the stunning Czech-Moravian highlands, through both urban and rural terrain, the route comprises an exhilarating mix of cycle paths, small streets, riverside trails and unmade tracks. It may take a while to fall in love with Brno – both the train and the bus station are scruffy, the signs to aid simple navigation are non-existent and there are skips full of rubble on every street – but the city's excellent public transport system is not only efficient, it also takes bikes. Maps are also freely available in every hotel lobby and tourist information point; the latest one details hills and some of the main cycle routes. If you are feeling energetic, a flurry of thigh-burning hills ups the ante between Tišnov and Doubravník through Lomnice. However, the journey is light on traffic, apart from the section that connects Doubravník with Nedvědice and a

Photo: Scotch Mist

breakneck stretch at Zouvalka opposite the Veveří castle – avoid this at all costs during the rush hour peaks.

Begin at Brno's FC Sparta stadium along the signposted routes of 1, 4 and 5 until joining the manicured cycle trails along the Svitava and Svratka rivers. This is where mountain bikers and road-racers compete each May on tracks that range from 100 kilometres (62 miles; road racers) and 55 kilometres (34 miles; mountain bikers) to a flat 30-kilometre (eighteen-mile) route for hobbyists. Follow the signs for Pernštejn via Hrad Veveří, Veverská Bítýška, Čebín and Lomnice – a picturesque little town situated seven kilometres (four miles) north of Tišnov reached through the Besének valley. Next, the riverside town of Doubravník leads to a fast-paced road into Nedvědice before a more leisurely, winding uphill slog to the castle of Pernštejn atop a rocky ledge. This beautifully fairy-tale setting dates back to the 13th century and is a much-used film location for period dramas. Cyclists keen not to experience their own mini-drama should watch out for razor-like rock chippings in and around the castle – it's wise to also keep a couple of reliable puncture kits to hand. Despite the installation of CCTV at every bike stand, cycle theft is a common nuisance, so it also pays to invest in a decent U-lock to secure your bike, even if you're not leaving it for long.

To help locate side streets with minimum traffic and the quietest backroads, avoiding maniacal intersections, check out the online Brno cycling map (www.brnonakole. cz), which marks local cycling paths and routes. Czech cycle app Cykloplánovač is also a useful tool because it details the elevation, type of road surface and traffic volume on specific routes city-wide. If roughshod woodland trails are more your thing, then head to the forests in northern and western Brno. Bike hire shops are plentiful and generally offer second-hand Dutch bikes for everyday riding around the city. For cycling further afield, the models are a little sportier to cope with the Tuscany-like terrain of southern Moravia and beyond. Take a train to Břeclav (where there are also plenty of bike rental options) and head out to Hrušovany u Brna, Vranovice, Popice or Březí to explore the famous biking trails that lead through vineyards and rolling green pasture. You can even stay overnight on a farm, campsite or family-run winery B&B to enjoy a leisurely Czech breakfast of warm yeast rolls, rye bread, homemade fruit jams, local cheese, fresh eggs and sliced salami – the perfect fuel for the long, hard climbs of the Moravian wine-lands.

Best time to visit? Well the weather is ideal for cycling any time from April to October. Street festivals characterise late May and early June, when fireworks light up the night-time city. Temperatures drop dramatically from October and the winters can be harsh. Hotels get very pricey during the MotoGP race weekend (usually the third weekend of August), so it pays to avoid this event, unless you are a fan of motorsports, as the roads are chaotic, there are queues at every restaurant and empty roads for cyclists are scarce.

Endurance level: Easy–Moderate

Tip: Tried a local dish you enjoyed? Ask the waiter to write down the name – it makes ordering it again a breeze.

Contacts:
Brno Tourist Information Centre
www.ticbrno.cz/en

Czech Tourist Board
www.czechtourism.com

STORK TRAIL, POLAND

Cyclists who are enthusiasts of nature will adore Poland's Stork Trail, a fascinating foray through foliage-flanked routes that promise plenty of sightings of birdlife and mammals. Every leaf seems to rustle, every hedgerow wriggles and trees seem alive with chirping, fluttering and squawking. As the name suggests, this ride is home to Poland's much-revered nesting birds, the stork.

Every fourth stork in the world comes from Poland, claim the locals. Certainly, few other countries, if any, can boast of more nesting birds of this species. Recent estimates suggest that there are as many as 40,900 pairs of storks nesting on Polish territory, with almost all choosing undisturbed habitat in the north-east and east of the country.

When they arrive, in late March, it heralds the onset of spring, which after the long, dark Polish winter is greeted with considerable glee. The storks have undergone a long, hard slog and journeyed well over 8,000 kilometres (4,971 miles) in four months to reach Europe. Storks rebuild their nests each year, with the male taking the lead. He brings all building material to the female – sticks, branches, earth, hay, bits of paper, strips of thread, scraps of fabric and tufts of dried grass. The female dutifully arranges everything to create an outer casing and inner lining, building an oval or elliptic nest, on poles or on roofs high above ground, anything up to two metres (six and a half feet) in diameter. Great care is taken with construction so that nests are robust and strong enough to take to large parents, eggs and nestlings. Storks begin to lay eggs in late April and hatching begins in the second half of May. By the end of July the young have left their parents' care. In between, they are fed by their carnivore parents – small invertebrates and tiny mammals, usually. Once they have started hunting for themselves, storks are eating rodents, moles, fish and small amphibians. The structure of food depends mainly on spatial and periodical diversity of a specific food type. Within a month, the young storks are ready to leave Poland for Africa, gathering in massive flocks (gaggles) of hundreds of birds that fly, feed and rest together. Storks are monogamous for a season, but part when it is time to migrate. The next year, they'll come back and form a different pairing: a powerful internal GPS brings them back to within 26 kilometres (sixteen miles) of their previous home. Their departure, to Polish observers, announces the end of summer.

Storks have been present in Polish folk culture for centuries, in superstitions, folklore and songs. When a stork nests on a particular rooftop, it is believed to bring the homeowner good luck and prosperity and to protect the house from lightning strike. Because they feed on pests such as rats, storks are valued as beneficial animals and their presence is celebrated as a force for good. Even in villages that are home to the country's largest stork breeding colonies – where humans are outnumbered by birds – residents wait for the storks' return each year to reclaim their pasture, farmlands and wetlands. Without the massive, tousled nests that balance precariously on telegraph poles, tree stumps, on top of chimneys, rooftops and specially made platforms, the village feels incomplete. Sometimes, numbers of storks are so high that nests are wedged into tree branches and balanced above electrical wires: the white eagle may be the symbol of Polish nationhood, but it is undoubtedly the white stork that holds the heart of Polish people. As long as the lakes aren't drained and the marshes remain untroubled by

Photo: MAREI.RU

development, the storks will continue to undertake this vast migratory trail to these fertile feeding grounds set among verdant, undulating hills.

Begin your journey in Gdańsk, Poland's historic seaport and the birthplace of Solidarity, the trade union movement headed by Lech Wałęsa that led to the end of Communist control of the country in 1989. From here, travel north-east to Frombork, a Gothic city where Nicolaus Copernicus lived from 1510 to 1543. It was in Frombork that he made his observations that the Earth rotates around the Sun. Next it is Żywkowo, barely a blip on the map and just a few skips from the Russian border, where a population of stork-lovers devote their lives to Poland's cherished birds – indeed, there's a man here who has been hailed as King of Storks for his stork museum; an outbuilding behind his home. Elsewhere in Żywkowo you'll find educational displays about the behaviour of storks in the area as well as a grand stork-viewing tower. One of the most impressive exhibits in the stork museum is an old nest of a mammoth size: nine feet tall and six feet in diameter, weighing around 500 pounds. With wingspans up to six feet, and gangly long legs and red-orange beaks, storks are a rather bizarre sight and highly visible as they soar over farm fields and reed beds in search of food. As the stork capital of Poland, this tiny village, in conjunction with the Polish Society for the Protection of Birds, attracts many thousands of stork tourists to rural Poland.

In 2001, Dwór Pentowo was awarded the status of European Stork Village by Euronatur, resulting in the launch of a designated Stork Trail cycle route that offers multi-day rides throughout the Podlasie region. An expert guide leads walking tours and manages a guesthouse for visiting stork nuts and with Zywkowo just four or five hours ride by bike from the budget airline hub of Gdańsk, via Dwór Pentowo (also on the Stork Trail), the 412.5-kilometre cycle trail is a great way to visit four national parks and witness the extraordinarily harmonious coexistence of stork and man. Weaving through some of Europe's most valuable natural habitat (dubbed the Polish Amazonia), the trail weaves through Białowieża (a UNESCO World Heritage Site, Poland's oldest National Park and the home of the largest herd of European bison), Biebrza, Narew and Wigry, with Dwór Pentowo itself well worth a visit as it is close to the Masurian Lake District and its spectacular 2,000 postglacial lakes.

Endurance level: Easy–Moderate

Tip: Feeling saddle-sore? The constant visual stimulation on this trip helps the miles pass by painlessly.

Contacts:
Poland National Tourist Board
www.poland.travel

Cycling Poland
www.cyclingpoland.com

CARPATHIAN MOUNTAINS, ROMANIA

Cycling across Romania's Carpathian Mountains is to plough through damp, flower-decked meadows to reach hilltop ridges high above narrow valleys. Skinny tracks no wider than an ironing board cut through tall, spiky ferns and spiral down steep-sided slopes covered in dark brooding forests. There, among the dense, silent woodlands and a confetti of tiny leaves, you'll ride across small exposed patches of dried brown mud. Before you leave your tyre track, scour the earth for other imprints – a bird, a deer or a bear. Romania is home to the biggest population of wild bears in Europe and they have their home right here in the wilderness region of the Carpathian Mountains. Scrutinise the ground for large paw prints with tell-tale thick, short claws that bury into damp soil. Look for smudged, elongated prints: only a few are perfectly paw-shaped. The inner toe in the track is the smallest and bears can walk plantigrade or flat-footed. They also place their feet in exactly the same place every time they use the same trail, so signs of footfall can be a depression worn into the ground by the passage of several bears over generations. Otherwise bears tend to leave very light impressions – the best prints are in dry, dusty soil when details of the pads can be seen.

As the strong and agile shy kings of Romanian mountains, bears can reach up to 48 kilometres per hour (30 miles per hour) in short, powerful bursts if they need to – considerably faster than most cyclists can manage on a bike.

Bears are usually nocturnal, but can also be active during the day. They spend most of their time eating and will nibble on practically anything: grass, leaves, nuts, berries, buds, twigs, roots, corn, fruits, insects, plants, invertebrates, fish, carrion, eggs, birds, small mammals and human rubbish. They will even dig up an underground wasp nest and gobble up it up whole – nest, buzzing insects and all. During the harshest winter months they hibernate, emerging once the weather warms up in spring. Several days before entering the den for winter, bears will consume only roughage, such as dry leaves. This forms a plug up to 30 centimetres (one foot) long in the digestive system that relaxes once winter is over. Bears may be reclusive, but their droppings are easier to spot as tubular scat over an inch wide. How it looks varies, depending on the diet of the animal. The poop I ride over appears to be 95 per cent berries and 5 per cent fur: a bit like a hairy piece of fruit candy retrieved from the back of a sofa.

Romania's European population of brown bears (*Ursus arctos*) totals about 6,000 at last tally, all of them inhabiting the Carpathian region. With its fast-flowing streams, cool air and bountiful crops of berries and bog rhubarb – both gastronomic delicacies to a brown bear – the deepest reaches of these glorious wild mountains are a bear haven. Many areas of the Carpathian Mountains see few visitors, Romanian or foreign, so the wildlife there is undisturbed. It may be less than a day's drive from Bucharest, but it may as well be another planet.

Only one cycle-touring company combines gentle bike rides through the mountains' giant rhubarb forests with bear spotting. Bike Romania runs bespoke cycle excursions and knows every inch of the quiet roads, flanked by trees of sour cherry and trailing vines and through hills and valleys steeped in folkloric magic and mystery. Bubbling hot springs, believed to have restorative powers, offer a promise of eternal youth, gurgle underground and spout forth among the rocks. It is not unusual for such claims to be made for the properties of some springs and wells in the region; plenty of handwritten signs urge those passing by to 'drink happily this water for it is good and clean and wets a thirsty mouth' – a real boon for cyclists.

Rough country roads to high ridges in the Carpathian Mountains require a keen use of the lowest gears. In a single morning, you may pass a solitary smallholding: rustic wooden houses wedged into woodlands with a pig, a cow, two dogs and a flock of hens. The scenery is meditative:

Photo: JoMa

peaceful, hushed with splendid views across magnificent lowland valleys untouched by time. The cycle path snakes up the slopes, twisting and turning through glades of spruce and oak to a mountain meadow that tumbles back down over the valley. A bear weighing up to half a tonne has been seen close by in a forest clearing. I shift up a gear and push the pedal with extra might, rather than encounter another shuffling brown figure with his nose in the air. It's amazing what makes a cyclist achieve top speed – I practically fly over the rutted footpath. An extraordinary sight greets me: natural gas fumaroles spouting yellow jets skywards like a mythical faraway land of Merlin. As well as bears and geothermal wells, the forest shelters boars, wolves, rare flowers, hundreds of birds and butterflies. On this traffic-free ride through the remote mountains of Romania, time really does seem to stand still – unless, that is, a bear just happens to pop up right in front of you and your bike.

According to the *Beginners' Guide to Bear Spotting*, there are important rules to follow when faced with a bear in the wild. Rule one: when exploring bear country, make a noise to alert the animals to your presence. Rule two: if confronted by a bear, do not turn and run. Rule three: if attacked, curl up in a ball and protect your face. And rule four: abandon rules one to three at the first sign of trouble – and pedal like heck.

The surprise and shock of catching sight of a bear at close quarters stalls my breathing. My bike halts, my body locks, my heart stops and I'm rooted to the saddle. The bear sniffs the air suspiciously, snuffles around in the leaf litter and slowly ambles away. Heart pounding, I cycle on in disbelief. It's been said before, but bear-watching in Romania is not 'a trip to the circus' – bears are numerous enough to stumble across among the jagged limestone, sweeping meadows and forested idyll dotted with blue orchids and buttercups. Bears here are as wild as the several-thousand species of plant. I'm thrilled to have seen a wild bear, on its own turf. Of course I am. Even that close to my front wheel. However, I realise – a little too late perhaps – that much of the fun is in the looking for, not the finding.

Endurance level: Moderate

Tip: Watch out for curious brown bears foraging for food in thick foliage, especially in the spring.

Contacts:
Romania Tourist Board
www.romania.travel

Cycling Romania
www.cyclingromania.ro

ADRIATIC CYCLEWAY, ITALY

Cycling along the wave-trimmed Adriatic Cycleway (Ciclovia Adriatica) gives you a real sense of what it must be to create a labour of love, because this 131-kilometre cycle-path – the longest of Italy's cycle routes – has been the brainchild of a group of passionate cyclists. Though it deviates inland and upland here and there, to the hinterland and uphill ridges, most of the route is along the coastline. The towns it runs through read like a shopping list of two-dozen exotic Italian ingredients – and this coastal jaunt is every bit as delectable as it sounds. Beginning in Martinsicuro to the south of the mouth of the Tronto River and weaving in and around Alba Adriatica, Tortoreto Lido, Giulianova, Roseto degli Abruzzi, Pineto and the Marine Protected Area of Cerrano you can catch a glimpse of the vivid underwater oasis that spreads seven kilometres (four miles) along the coast. Next it's past the tree-lined sands of Silvi Montesilvano, Pescara, Francavilla Al Mare, Ortona, Costa Dei Trabocchi and the mid-sea wooden fishing platforms 'La Costa dei Trabocchi' at San Vito Chietino before reaching San Salvo – the very last Abruzzo town on the Adriatic coast.

From Martinsicuro in the province of Teramo, the road skirts along some mesmerising coastline and it is a joy to whiz along during a breezy morning, brightened by a golden egg-yolk sun. Next it's the neat, tufted wine terraces of Notaresco and its renowned Nicodemi winery. The trio of wines from this family-owned 38-hectare (94-acre) organic vineyard in the Montepulciano d'Abruzzo appellation have been produced with considerable devotion. The nutty dry white is light and very drinkable and the spicy red has a dense raspberry flavour. Once my waistband has tightened after consuming salted olives, crumbly white cheese and crusty fresh bread, and the wine has begun to tickle my eyelids, it's time to jump back on the saddle. After weaving through the bumpy roads in the village of Montepagano, it is back out onto the seaside road where I'm grateful for hair-raising blasts of fresh sea air. Signs direct me to the umbrella-scattered sands of Roseto degli Abruzzi, where I'm staying overnight.

After a wholesome breakfast of smoked Abruzzo sausages and hams, I pound the pedals with extra vigour towards the beautiful village of Atri with its flower-filled balconies, bloom-topped baskets and neat little stone-built houses. Lunch is Torano sausage and special liver sausage preserved in oil with pale-white mozzarella that sets me up for the ride to Città Sant'Angelo, which is characterised by 18th-century brick houses perched on a hill overlooking the Saline River valley and is considered one of Italy's prettiest villages. It is indeed lovely: an endearing place with charming courtyards overspilling with crimson flowers and vines trailing over trellises. I shift up to top gear for the rapidly tumbling roads back to the shore-side route and enjoy a salty-aired freewheel descent to the coast in time to reach Montesilvano in time for a dinner of fine Pescarse seafood with Fettuccine.

It's another bright morning sky as I bid Montesilvano 'arrivederci' and point the bike in the direction Pescara, a fishing town reached via the architecturally resplendent Ponte del Mare, a fine sea bridge. From here it is a meander up, down and around hills to the historic sea-front town of Ortona, a settlement with picture-perfect blue waters, white buildings and cream-coloured cliffs. Delve into just-wide-enough winding alleys within the old part of town to discover bars, restaurants and ice cream parlours. The scene of fierce fighting over the centuries, Ortona owes its survival to its towering cliff-walls, old fortified castle and strong defences. From here, it's a scenic ride along a disued railway line full of butterflies and birds to the 28-hectare (59-acre) Punta dell'Acquabella reserve and its beautiful pocket-sized sandy beach. It is the sort of place that makes your heart sing with its skinny streets, alleyways and little paved corners covered in potted plants. Flowers and washing hang from rickety balconies above me as I idly watch the fishing boats unloading their haul. I overnight in San Vito Chietino and lose myself in a stunning panoramic view surrounding mountains and dark moon-speckled waters that are home to submerged fishing nets and vast shoals of silvery fish.

The next day, I ride across terrain that saw action in the

Photo: paulox_net

Second World War, including the ancient Gustav line where in 1943 the Germans erected a staunch bulwark towards the Allied offensive. I keep my head down close to the handlebars as the small, rounded hills are being lashed by a strong wind. The landscape opens up before me like the turning pages of a history book as a succession of relics provide tell-tale clues to its past. Invaders who arrived here over the centuries include the ancient Greeks, the Romans, the Byzantines, the Normans, Emperor Fredrick II and the Spanish Bourbons. Amid the rolling wheat fields, coastal plains, salty sands, dunes and olive groves, this region has witnessed pilgrimage and plunder for well over a thousand years. White-painted towns cling to hillsides surrounded by criss-crosses of crumbling drystone walls in a land blessed with a sublime climate, easy roads and incredible food. I marvel at the daubs of colour in the sky, spreading like ink on blotting paper. Italy's wonderful sunsets have come up trumps again: providing a spectacular kaleidoscopic ending to another perfect day on two wheels.

Endurance level: Moderate

Tip: Invest in a padded saddle for this ride; the bumps on the road are bum-bruisers.

Contacts:
Italy Tourist Board
www.italiantouristboard.co.uk

Italy Cycling Guide
www.italy-cycling-guide.info

VENETIAN LAGOON, ITALY

If reclining in a gondolier in Venice while someone else does all the work just isn't your style, then the rewards of sightseeing the Venetian Lagoon on a bike may be the way to go. Away from one of the world's most urban conurbations, Venice's ecologically blessed crescent-shaped body of water begs to be explored. Set within the clasp-like grip of three grabs of land – Litorale Pellestrina, Litorale di Lido and Litorale del Cavallino – the Laguna Véneta's 45-kilometre (28-mile) expanse comprises weed-fringed marshy river-fed lowlands flushed by the saline waters of the Adriatic. Slow-moving tidal flows and mysterious currents wash past shifting sandbanks and deep basins into salt-water pastures rich in crabs, shrimp, mussels, limpets, octopus and squid. Nesting gulls, herons, spoonbills, swans, snipe and ducks hide among vegetation-cloaked shallows. Even mullet and sea bass thrive around the islands in the lagoon.

Cycle paths offer that right-by-the-water fascination as they run around an inch away from the edge of Venice lagoon. While the city of Venice is famously tilting to the east because of subsidence, the sea-level is also rising ever-so-slightly each year. Land is also shifting in Venice's lagoon – all 117 islands seem to be dropping at an annual rate of about a couple of millimetres. One reason is that the Adriatic plate, on which Venice sits, is sub-ducting beneath the Apennines Mountains. Sediments beneath the city are also becoming more compact. In truth, the beautiful World Heritage site of Venice has been flooding since the 10th century. Now, with 22 million tourists visiting the city every year, greater efforts are being made to bring the beauty of

Photo: Jean-Pierre Dalbéra

the wider lagoon area to international attention. Venice, say the locals, is much more than a single city – and as you pedal around the bird-filled waters that lap the islands you get a sense of how much this is true.

Wildlife has long found the gorges, crevices and fertile tidal sands a hospitable place to settle and include an abundance of species such as swifts, starlings, pigeons and bats. As one of Europe's most important humid wetland areas, the region attracts a large number of wintering, nest-building and non-migratory species that feed on the shrimp, sea roach, clams, periwinkles, worms, snails and squid. Sea fennel and sea lavender thrive in the brackish water and there are dandelions, Bermuda grass flourishing in among the cracks between the stones. Mussels and barnacles can also be found attached to seaweeds and semi-submerged wood. In the muddiest parts of the water, you'll find green crab. During low tide, the waters reveal sea anemones, squirts and sponges. Tides are influenced by the tidal waters of the Upper Adriatic Sea and expose mudflats and sand-flats in the shallow estuary known as the 'Queen of the Adriatic': the largest wetland in the Mediterranean consisting of saltwater marshes and thin barrier islands. A trio of narrow openings to the Adriatic, and two large rivers – the Sile and the Brenta – that empty into the lagoon, form the basis of the coastal waters that make up Italy's largest lagoon.

Protected by the Lidos of Venice and Pellestrina, the Venetian Lagoon's cycle paths hug these natural levees to allow bikes to meander to the south. The route snakes along flat roads and involves boarding a ferry to access some stretches, for example to reach Chioggia at the lagoon's southern tip, passing old sea walls and waters dotted with ramshackle fishermen's huts on stilts strewn with mussel nets. The walls extend for miles in a robust piece of engineering completed in the dying days of the Venetian Republic. Chioggia is a miniature Venice, filled with cobblestone streets, canals and a well-known fish market. Take the snaking loop to the Po Delta and back to clock up about 54 kilometres (34 miles) in total from the city centre, a scenic and exhilarating journey that's doable in around six hours.

A special waterbus service links San Giuliano, the Venice Lido and Punta Sabbioni to the island of Sant' Erasmo, where gentle cycling allows for a meander through some spectacular flower-filled countryside. The waterbus has enough space for 60 bikes, so pre-booking/pre-paying is advisable at any of Venice's many Vela ticket offices and agencies. The service runs on weekends and public holidays only, with return tickets 9.30 Euros, including passenger and bike. A room in one of Chioggia's decent handful of hotels along the seaside Sottomarina Lido provides a restful overnight stop.

Nothing defines Venice's cuisine like its seafood: you'll find a fresh haul of sea creatures from the surrounding lagoon on every menu. Fish is sold daily once the boats have returned to shore so that anchovies, razor clams, cuttlefish, squid, monkfish and mussels can be served simply in Venetian restaurants together with a true speciality, soft shell crab. Caught young, the crabs – called moleche by Venetians – are only available for a few weeks in spring and autumn. And in Europe, these tasty crustaceans can only be found in the northern part of the Venetian lagoon.

Venice's fish market on the Rialto, a 1,000-year-old institution, sells this uniquely Venetian crab rarity. Timing is very important in order to catch the crabs after they have shed their shell, so there is an art to crab fishing. The molecanti – as the moleche fishermen of the Venetian lagoon are called – work from five fisheries that have been operating at the lagoon for more than 300 years. To enjoy a plate of soft shell crabs cooked the local way, be sure to visit the canal-side lagoon restaurant, Trattoria al Gatto Nero da Ruggero on the northern island of Burano. It's the perfect meal to end a day cycling on the edge of the lagoon.

Endurance level: Easy–Moderate

Tip: Don't be tempted to ride here after sundown, even with lights. Save your miles for the safety of daylight.

Contacts:
Cycling Venice Lagoon
www.cyclingvenicelagoon.com

Venetian Tourist Board
www.turismovenezia.it

LAONA TO AKAMAS, CYPRUS

To cycle in Cyprus is to journey the maritime crossroads of the eastern Mediterranean basin, through a rich and varied history of mariners, marauders, settlers and invaders that include the Greeks, Romans, Byzantines, Lusignans, Genoese, Venetians, Ottomans, British and Turks. Inhabited by humans since the Aceramic Neolithic period (*c.*10,000 BC) when the comedic-looking Pleistocene-era pygmy hippopotamus and dwarf elephant still roamed the island, a major era for development and prosperity was when the first Greek settlers established a series of city kingdoms across the north, centre and south of the island.

Cyprus was annexed by the expanding Roman Empire in 58 BC and enjoyed six centuries of relative peace and development. Today, the evidence of Christianity and Islam is found in crumbling white-stone churches, grand fresco-adorned monasteries and elaborate mosques. The Venetians built mammoth fortifications and immense circular walls, the Ottomans shared land wealth between rural communities, the British built military bases to establish a Middle Eastern hub and the independent Republic of Cyprus was realised in 1960. Political instability and social unrest persisted between the Greek-Cypriot and Turkish-Cypriot communities, culminating in the 1974 division of Cyprus. Relations have significantly improved in recent years, with frontiers between the north and south of Cyprus relaxed and cross-border travel encouraged. Regardless of separation, all Cypriots remain proudly patriotic about their homeland – both Turkish and Greek – with younger generations keen for reunification.

Despite being the third-largest island in the Mediterranean, to cycle across this ancient isle is relatively easy due to its compact size. Old stone villages are strung together by dry stone walls in close succession and numerous dramatic topographical contrasts ensure it feels like travelling a whole continent condensed. Though Cyprus is renowned for its rugged beaches, some of its lesser known landscapes are equally spectacular, such as the pine-clad peaks, eucalyptus forests, vineyards, olive and citrus groves. Magnificent ancient ruins appear at every turn and include the ancient city-kingdom of Kourion, a mosaic-rich amphitheatre for gladiatorial games and Amathous, an important place for worship of Aphrodite. For cyclists, this means a wide variety of different road surfaces across a rapidly changing terrain that offers plenty of visual excitement.

Photo: Dmitry Panow

Cyprus is now so popular with adventurous two-wheelers that the Cyprus Tourism Organisation has started to create a national cycling network with signposted routes to follow in rural areas. This has spawned a growing number of bicycle shops offering cycle guides for mountain bike and road cyclists along peaceful lanes and traffic-free trails where the only hazards are wild donkeys and grazing goats. Numerous well-stocked bike rental outlets stock serious road-racing pro kits, including a variety of SCOTT Carbon and Aluminium models and a wide range of helmets and shoes. You'll find that bikes are properly equipped with clipless pedals, a water bottle and a saddle bag with extra inner tube and multi-tool inside. If you plan to use your own gear, be sure to treat it to a full pre-trip MoT because Cyprus's backroads are unforgiving. Pack a bike vest, puncture repair kit, map, windproof jacket, first aid kit, helmet, lots of sun protection, cycling shoes, bug spray and a good quality hydro-pack.

On even the shortest trip in Cyprus, it isn't uncommon to encounter rocky tracks, clay trails, quiet country backroads and slick, flat busier asphalt. Some of the most thrilling uphill rides are courtesy of the mountain climbs in the Troodos, Machairas or Akamas region, where you'll find cycling world champions training in winter, including Gold Olympic Medallist Jaroslav Kulhavý. A jam-packed competitive racing calendar, organised by the Cyprus Cycling Federation (a member of the International Cycling Union) has existed on the island since 1978. Yet thousands of people cycle Cyprus without aiming for a medal: they simply enjoy pounding the pedals with the wind in their hair, the sun on their back, the gentle crunch of tyres on gravel and the sounds of nature all around with resplendent views of the sparkling sea.

One of my favourite routes is one that follows an age-old pathway from Laona to Akamas in the north-western flank of Cyprus as it weaves its way through tufted vineyards and five independent wineries where visitors are encouraged to stop and try. The route, which snakes along secondary roads (mainly on the E701 and E709) boasts a steady ascent past vines, pasture and flower-filled shrubs and bushes up to a bird-filled forest. From here, sleepy milk-stone villages cling to a landscape seemingly unchanged by time in among centuries-old olive groves. Every few miles you'll pass a traditional Cypriot tavern, where the hosts ensure a warm welcome. What's more, the landscape is spectacular: a colour-rich panorama of scenery, cultural, geographic and geological interest that slowly unfurls as you pedal. Meander off on narrow tracks to discover grassy knolls shaded by giant trees, valley views and small meze restaurants keen to share the pleasures of their kitchens.

Visiting in August? Then you'll have the chance to celebrate in local style during the Dionysia Grape Festival. Held on the route, roughly mid-way in the village of Stroumbi, the festival honours Dionysus, the Greek god of wine. Since 1967, the annual 'Dance of the Grape' has wowed an audience in the cobbled village square; today, the festival lasts three whole days and attracts people from all over the region. Enjoy traditional costumes, folk dancing, Cypriot music and a chance to sample dozens of home-grown red, white and rose wines and lots of regional foods.

The best cycling weather in Cyprus is found in the months between October and April, when temperatures range between 15°C and 25°C – avoid exposed roads during the hottest months of July and August unless you plan to stick to the higher, coolest parts of the Troodos Mountains. You'll see more wildlife and brightly coloured wildflowers and greenery if you visit February to May.

Endurance level: Difficult

Tip: Invest in fitted eyewear to keep the dust and grit at bay on this trip.

Contacts:
Bikin' Cyprus Adventures
www.bikincyprusadventures.com

Cyprus Tourist Board
www.visitcyprus.com

MOUNT ARARAT, TURKEY

The peaks of Mount Ararat figure in both the Christian and Islamic faiths, appearing in the pages of the Bible and the Koran. Followers of both religions know it as the place where Noah's Ark came to rest after the flood. As the vessel in which God spares Noah, his family and a chosen pair of all the world's animals, the ark had been built entirely of wood by Noah. After floating, in safety, throughout the pounding rains and rising floodwater, the ark, Noah and his menagerie appears as Safina Nuh in the Koran (meanings Noah's boat) and teba (meaning ark) in the Bible.

Numerous expeditions have scoured the peaks in search of the ark – the earliest on record was around AD 275 – with many more as recently as the 1950s and 1970s. However, no scientific evidence exists for a flood on such a global scale or such a salvation from waters. And despite forensic efforts, no sign of the 137-metre (450-foot) vessel has been found. Closely paralleling the cyclical story of creation, from the creation to the un-creation and subsequent re-creation, scholars suggest that the nine known versions of the Mesopotamian flood story provide a basic plot for all subsequent flood-stories and heroes, including Noah. Modern travellers continue to be fascinated by the mystery and myth associated with the storied peaks: a dormant volcano that soars 5,165 metres (16,946 feet) into the clouds, it shows no sign of erupting, although an earthquake did cause devastation in 1840.

Located at Agri, in eastern Turkey near the borders with Armenia and Iran, Mount Ararat is served by a road that runs to Iran through to Doğubayazıt, a transit town just south of Ararat. Snowy upper peaks rarely ever thaw and the last hundred metres are permanently ice. Soot-coloured basalt rocks the size of double-decker buses cover the lower and middle slopes. Brooding shadows add to the intrigue of a mountain so rich in ancient fables and accounts by Marco Polo. Allah describes the ark as 'a thing of boards and nails', telling Noah to build a boat shaped like a bird's belly from teak.

Rising in isolation above the surrounding plains and valleys and providing an enthralling panoramic view of Armenia, Iran and Turkey, the mountain is home to nomadic Kurds who tend their herds of cattle and sheep among its grass-tufted ledges. A smaller peak – Little Ararat (3,896 metres; 12,782 feet) – rises up on the south-east shoulder of the main mountain. This is inhabited by a god of fire, according to an age-old legend: a perfect being, except for the cosmic shakes he caused during rage-filled outbursts caused by an explosive temper. In times of anger, gusts would whistle through the crevices of the mountain like a fiery whirlwind, high above the valley. Once he mellowed, the god was assigned the task of tending to a newborn earth

Photo: Andrew Behesnilian

god. He protected the child, ensuring light and warmth over the cradle by controlling the rays of the sun. Today, though the mountain is cold, the foothills are warm and dusty, with the deserts of Iran just sixteen kilometres (ten miles) away. Grazing livestock nibble at the scrub that sprouts from the mountain's lava plateau. Vast areas of Mount Ararat were reshaped in 1840 by a major earthquake, particularly around the epicentre of Ahora Gorge, a dramatic chasm that drops 1,825 metres (6,000 feet).

From the transit-and-trading town of Doğubayazıt, a winding route heads out to Mount Ararat, skirting the lowest reaches of the mountain for about fifteen kilometres (nine miles). Depending on the weather, this journey along a track of rocks and loose-stone debris can take two or three hours. As a predominantly Kurdish city of around 35,000 people, Doğubayazıt has a rustic border-town wildness about it that is distinctly different from other parts of Turkey. Doğubayazıt was once a key staging post on a vital ancient trade route from Trabzon to north-western Iran. Its role has diminished since trade along this route declined during the Russo-Turkish wars of the 19th century and the First World War, when Russian troops occupied the town.

Amongst rocky foothills, set in a stark treeless plain, it feels a long, long way from Ankara (an eighteen-hour drive) or Istanbul (34 hours by car). In truth, geographically and spiritually, you are not just on the road to Iran but already in the Middle East. Yet Doğubayazıt's setting is superb and starting the adventure in this busy mountain town (at around 1,800 metres; 5,906 feet) forms part of the whole Mount Ararat experience. Doğubayazıt may lack charm, with its smoky cafes and rubble, but a constant buzz of activity and the comings and goings of travellers, merchants and passers-through sprinkles a little romance on the grit.

Few Turkish towns boast such a heavenly location, wedged between the talismanic peaks that hold court over the landscape and the grandeur of the splendid İshak Paşa Palace. Set on a small plateau beneath stark cliffs, this magnificent dome-topped mansion combines Ottoman, Seljuk, Georgian, Persian and Armenian architectural influence. Commissioned in 1685 by an Ottoman general, the palace was completed in 1784 and early in the 1930s stood in the town of Eski Bayazıt. However, this town was demolished by the Turkish army after a Kurdish uprising, leading to the founding of modern Doğubayazıt. Be sure to set aside enough time to enjoy a stroll through the first courtyard, past dungeons and gardens to a second courtyard. Ornate mosaics and elegant stairs leads to the palace's selamlık (men's quarters) and haremlık (women's quarters). There are also ceremonial courtyards, a handsome mosque and some carvings, fine Persian decoration, intricate stonework and elaborate ceiling frescoes. The gold-plated doors, masterpieces of Kurdish craftsmanship, were removed by Russian troops at their retreat from Anatolia in 1917 and are apparently now found on display in St Petersburg's Hermitage Museum. To the castle's right stands the striped-stone tomb of Ahmad Khani, a beloved 17th-century Kurdish poet and philosopher. And all the time, the peaks of Mt Ararat are lording over you, proud, tall and erect.

To travel in a land blessed with such an extensive history is a curious adventure. In the foothills, it is hard not to keep all eyes peeled for a remnant of Noah's great boat – even as you're navigating a pothole the size of a minivan. In the 1950s, a Frenchman claimed to have found a piece of the ark's decking, but carbon dating showed the wood to be too young. I scrutinise every log and splintered branch that I pass, just to be certain it isn't an important relic. The road is roughshod and soon I yearn for a cushion for my cycling shorts. Yet I push on, thankful for several spare inner tubes, keen to reach the highest point of Mount Ararat I can without dismounting. I manage to hit around 2,500 metres (8,202 feet) before the road peters out to nothing after gradually disintegrating over a good couple of hours. I'm as far as I can go by bike. Am I disappointed? Not one bit. I have learned never to feel cheated when I cannot ride up to the summit. And at Mount Ararat, wobbling precariously from the foothills to the middle slopes feels like enough of a challenge. Thunder is echoing around the valley and it is roaring like a bomb-blast, which I take as a cue to tackle the descent. I ride upright, high out of the saddle for comfort to save my bruised posterior from more rigour. The Turks call the mountain Agri Dagi (Mountain of Pain) and Kurds refer to it as the Ciyaye Agiri (Mountain of Fire): I wonder if that has anything to do with exploring the sheer, steep bumpy trail by bike?

Endurance level: Difficult

Tip: Be prepared for waves, cheers and offers of hospitality – cyclists are a rare sight here!

Contact:
Turkey Tourist Board
www.goturkeytourism.com

TRANS-SIBERIAN HIGHWAY, RUSSIA

Cycling the biggest country in the world is as epic as it sounds: Russia is a vast expanse of land. To cross it, you and your saddle will do a journey of roughly 16,000 kilometres (9,940 miles), across eleven time zones and two continents. Most of it will be on unlit, bum-bruising potholed roads. Russia's courteous, friendly drivers (the sober ones) more than make up for the cheek-numbing discomfort, as I discovered when I decided to ride the Trans-Siberian Highway. They wave. They shout 'Zdravstvuite!' (hello) warmly. They bring you bowls of soup. And pass you crumpled notes of relatives to call on for an overnight rest stop. Spanning the width of Russia, from the Baltic Sea that extends from the Atlantic Ocean to the Pacific Ocean's Sea of Japan, the Trans-Siberian Highway isn't actually an official road but a network of federal highways. If it were a single road, it would rival Australia's Highway 1 as the longest on the planet, stretching from the golden domed grandeur of St Petersburg to Golden Horn Bay in Vladivostok, near the borders with China and North Korea: a mammoth route on which cyclists are welcomed on every stretch.

Cycling all the way from Siberia to the Pacific Ocean raises some key basic concerns: freezing temperatures, roughshod roads, vodka-swigging drivers and some bitter easterly headwinds of enormous might that rage full-force against the bike. Siberian tigers and fearsome bears are also cause for considerable alarm. Yet the most worrisome wildlife on the journey aren't the 700-pound carnivorous wildcats but Eastern Siberian encephalitis-carrying ticks the size of a sesame seed. Resulting in sickness and nerve damage, this rare disease can even cause paralysis in humans, so an inoculation is a worthwhile precaution.

Vladivostok, situated in the south-east of Russia, is reachable via a mix of paved freeways, badly dinted asphalt and long stretches of pot-holed narrow dirt roads in Siberia's more remote parts. Improving the road surfaces to Vladivostok is an ongoing project, though most people doubt if the route to the Pacific Ocean will be a single, smooth highway before Hell freezes over. Construction projects along the route have spawned several legends over time. For example, an inexplicable semicircle of road is said to exist somewhere on an otherwise completely straight line. The explanation? That Joseph Stalin used a ruler to mark where the highway should pass and his pencil jumped over his finger. Because the engineers were under threat to make the segment exactly as commanded, they were too scared to deviate from Stalin's drawing, hence a strange curve nicknamed 'The Tsar's Finger'.

Today, cyclists can trace the route of the 'World's toughest bike race' on the whole 9,400 kilometres (5,841 miles) across Siberia, measuring distances in 1,448-kilometre (900-mile) chunks and changing a half-dozen flat tyres in a day, just like the Lycra-clad pros. The Red Bull Trans-Siberian Extreme makes the Tour de France, Giro d'Italia and Vuelta a España look positively lightweight, with fifteen stages and a total of 58 kilometres (36 miles) of climbing. Starting in the Russian capital city Moscow, the course broadly follows the route of the famous Trans-Siberian railway – much like my own Atlantic to Pacific ride – before finishing with the sorest rear imaginable in Vladivostok. By the time the participants toast their safe arrival with a neat Russian vodka, they'll have passed the Ural mountains, four of the world's longest rivers and experienced the diversity of peoples along the borders of Kazakhstan, Mongolia and China. They'll have covered a total of 79,000 metres (259,186 feet) of ascent and spent more than three weeks on the road. For comparison, the Race Across America (RAAM) covers approximately 4,800 kilometres (2,983 miles) to the Red Bull Trans-Siberian Extreme's 9,400 kilometres – a mere walk in the park. For anyone who likes a cycling challenge, it really is the ultimate ultra-marathon cycling event.

Striking scenery along the route becomes austere, desolate and stark in parts – but beautiful none the less. You'll also encounter potential temperature fluctuations of up to 40°C and hear dozens of different dialects as well as witness vast disparities in wealth.

From Moscow to the river tourism town of Nizhny Novgorod ('Nizhny'), the M-7 runs parallel to Europe's longest river, the Volga. Flowing through central Russia and into the Caspian Sea, the Volga has a special place in the hearts and minds of Russians as the country's national river: a 160-kilometre (99-mile) stretch with a sizeable drainage basin that includes as many as 500 channels and smaller rivers. The ride continues across the Nizhny Novgorod region, and the Chuvashia and Tatarstan Republics, past history-steeped architecturally unique Russian cities and towns, surrounded by picturesque landscapes. The road to Perm travels through three Russian regions – Tatarstan, Udmurtia and Perm Krai – and crosses more than 40 rivers. On the P-242 through the Sverdlovsk Region to Yekaterinburg, you'll cross the Europe–Asia border through the majestic Ural mountain peaks.

Venturing across the West Siberian Plain means crossing about fifteen rivers. Then it's a stretch alongside the rivers of Irtysh and Om before arriving in Russia's third-largest city, Novosibirsk. Riding to Krasnoyarsk reveals Siberia in all its splendour. Then it is on to Irkutsk along the P-255 highway,

Photo: ugraland

crossing more than twenty rivers, including the mighty Yenisei and the beautiful Angara. The route to Ulan-Ude is via the picturesque banks of the deepest freshwater lake on the Earth, Lake Baikal. Boasting the highest level of biodiversity, it is home to amazing flora and fauna, putting the lake on UNESCO's World Natural Heritage List. Next, it's along P-258 to Chita, which has a section alongside a major river, Selenga, which makes its way to Lake Baikal through Russia and Mongolia. From Chita, the route continues to Svobodny in the Amur region, a town with an extreme climate with monsoons, swinging temperatures and heavy rainfall in summer on a bumpy, climbing stretch that is one of the most painful stretches in the saddle. Next to Khabarovsk, before a triumphant 765-kilometre victory leg, finishing with a raised arm sprint into the port city of Vladivostok that sits on a peninsula jutting out into a gulf of the Sea of Japan.

Such an epic ride through thousands of miles of farmland, mountains, lakes, valleys, snow-kissed forests and dark woodlands makes it a difficult journey to pack for – the temperature variations alone necessitate everything from thin, cotton summer clothes to thermal layers and thick socks. Prepare for sweltering heat and ice and snow, and everything in between. The famous Siberian chill is felt most painfully in your extremities, so buy a decent thermal hat and high-quality gloves that offer protection down to –30°C. If you're planning to spend time around beautiful Lake Baikal, don't forget to pack insect repellent and a head net for lakeside hikes.

Endurance level: Difficult

Tip: Don't let unpredictable local weather catch you out – ask a local for the lowdown (they are never wrong …).

Contacts:
Russian Cycle Touring Club
www.rctc.ru

Red Bull Trans-Siberian Extreme
www.redbull.com/uk/en/bike/events

ASIA

KERALA, INDIA

Legions of adventure-seeking cyclists rave about the sheer thrill of riding through southern India – a stretch of land blessed with deep-blue waters flanked by foliage in a palette of vivid hues. Bouncing down long, bumpy descents turns the colourful view into a muddle of colourful, scenic pleasures. Women in bejewelled saris. Vibrant green shrubs by the roadside backdropped by giant palms. Ragged sands, wave-smoothed boulders and prehistoric-looking gigantic rocks characterise Hampi, while jewel-tone birdlife sends iridescent plashes through Munmar's lush, green hills and tufted thickets. Reaching the fishermen's villages on the coast takes you a world away from the chaos of India's larger towns. In rural Kerala, a region known for 900 kilometres (559 miles) of interconnected backwaters and canals, you'll find five sparkling lakes and 38 rivers. A mix of both freshwater and seawater waterways ensures Kerala has a unique ecosystem that is home to many species, including crabs, turtles, kingfishers and golden-tinged palms. Many of the rivers are small and entirely fed by monsoon rainfall.

Photo: Abbyabraham

Stretching along the Malabar Coast, and spanning 38,863 square kilometres (15,005 square miles), Kerala is shaped by the Lakshadweep Sea to the west. Fishermen, merchants, ferries and cargo freight have all plied these waters, with the first export departing Kerala ports in 3000 BC the region's fine dried and powdered spices. Many European settlers were attracted to the region by the maritime spice trade, including the Portuguese. Kerala has long been known as the 'Spice Garden of India', though coconuts, tea and cashews flourish too. A store-owner in a spice-stained overall tells me proudly that in the last ten years the world spice trade has grown to around 500,000 tonnes of spices – and that the major chunk, by far, is still from Kerala. As I ride through fields, my nose catches a warm scented breeze infused with cardamom, clove, cinnamon, ginger, turmeric, tamarind, nutmeg and curry leaves. I gulp it down and imagine a time when the pepper of Kerala reached Europe through the Arab traders. Europe saw great potential in pepper as a food preservative and looked for complete control on its trade. Colonial wars and conquests followed, such was the power of spice.

Another fascinating fact I learn is that Kerala was once almost entirely undersea. Once I know this, I scrutinise the ground more carefully and discover evidence of ancient marine fossils. In fact, some crunch underfoot on crumbling rocks and I later learn that Kerala is a recognised centre for archaeological excavations. With a humid tropical equatorial climate, Kerala has three climatically distinct regions: the eastern highlands, rugged and cool mountainous terrain; the central mid-lands, rolling hills; and the western lowlands, coastal plains. The highest peak in south India – Anamudi – shoots up over 2,695 metres (8,842 feet) in the east of the region, while the western swathe of Kerala's landscape is mostly flat (but I still manage to find a hill ...).

Rainy days a year run to around 120–140 in Southwest Kerala, with seasonal heavy rains common in the monsoon seasons. Around 65 per cent of the rainfall occurs from June to August; the rest falls from September to December. In eastern Kerala, a drier tropical wet and dry climate prevails, with gale force winds, storm surges, cyclone-related torrential downpours and occasional droughts in summer.

Over 25 per cent of India's 15,000 plant species are found in Kerala – a large number of them endemic or medicinal. Rice is grown everywhere in extensive paddy fields and you'll find more than 1,000 species of trees. Some of the world's most iconic wildlife species hide among the crops, foliage and tree cover, such as the Indian elephant, Bengal tiger, Indian leopard, giant grizzled squirrels, king cobra, viper, python and mugger crocodile. Elephants have long fulfilled an integral role in the culture of Kerala, where there is the largest domesticated population of elephants in India. Temples and wealthy landowners have around 700 domesticated elephants, which are kept mainly for ceremonial purposes and for the 10,000 or more colourful processions and elaborate displays at important state-wide festivals and celebrations.

Cyclists will soon discover that Kerala's 145,704 kilometres (90,536 miles) of roads vary dramatically, from the widespread erosion of backroads due to flooding to the traffic-worn-surfaces of much-used larger roads (vehicle density in the state is four times the national average). Kerala has narrower roads than the rest of India, which means cyclists can be pushed into the gutter by trucks and buses. Showers cause slippery conditions, leading to the highest number of road traffic accidents in the country. Sharp debris (nails, glass and scraps of metal) are constant threats to tyres and inner tubes, but thankfully there are plenty of places to get these nuisances fixed. Auto garages, cycle shops and even the local police station will happily help with mechanical failure and everyone seems to know someone who can patch tyres, replace brake pads, weld pedals and deal with multiple punctures. It pays to learn a few words of the local language: even the most basic level of communication can help a cyclist in trouble. Buy a map before you arrive in India because local maps are scarce and often out of date. Helmets and other gear are also in short supply.

In India it helps to ride a bike that melds into the local crowd (if it has a loud bell or horn to honk, even better – alerting other road users to your presence is vital for surviving the roads). Rattling lorries pass by so dangerously close you can feel the heat of the metal bodywork on your skin. Then, just for the heck of it, they blast a deafening siren that causes any cyclist to jump out of their skin. Oncoming traffic can be blinding because many of the big trucks have their lights permanently on full beam. Buses also barrel towards you at maximum velocity, utterly blind to the fact that there is a cycle in its path.

Endurance level: Moderate

Tip: Muscles aching? Try the local tea infusion. It contains a sage-like antispasmodic to soothe muscular aches and pains.

Contacts:
Cycling in India
www.cyclinginindia.com

Kerala Tourism
www.keralatourism.org

India Tourism
www.incredibleindia.org

KHARDUNG LA, INDIA

To hit the world's highest motorable road on 20 pounds of lightweight alloy is almost certainly a form of insanity, yet each year several hundred cyclists do just that. The Khardung La in India may be just 45 kilometres (28 miles) long, but it is a stretch deprived of all but a lungful of oxygen: the cycling starts at 5,602 metres (18,380 feet) above sea level, along narrow, mountainous pathways. A weather-beaten milestone at the very top of the rocks informs you how high you are, confirming what the nausea has already confirmed. It's ironic that the views from a bike seat along the Khardung La are utterly breathtaking, yet there isn't a breath to take ...

Riding this crazy mountain pass is, well, terrifying: the adrenaline kicks in moments before your stomach hits your feet and the wind whips your hair into a frenzy. Above, the heavens feel close enough to touch; below the world is at your feet. On a bike, exposed to the elements and physically connected to every shake, rattle and roll of the road, the thrill of this route is almost overwhelming. Through the pedals, every inch of the character of Ladakh's landscape is felt deeply, while the weather and stunning beauty is realised through your skin and eyes. Gateway to the Shyok and Nubra valleys, Khardung La (meaning, the Khardung Pass in Tibetan) lies 37 kilometres (23 miles) north of the city of Leh. Most cyclists pick up their mountain bike and

Photo: Samson Joseph

helmet from tour guides here who organise cycling trips for adventure freaks. They promise a real test of cycling at high altitude and woo you with gorgeous photographs of Khardung La and its scenery. Only cyclists with stamina and courage (or delusions) enlist to climb up to the dizzying height of the 'K-top', where stark, sheer drops feel inches away from the loose-stone path as fierce winds slap around your face. Keep your gloves on, even if your palms feel sweaty, because the air can easily numb your fingers enough to make it hard to brake.

Cyclists of good general fitness will take several hours to reach the top and there's a growing trend for cycle tour companies to ferry you to the summit in order to enjoy traversing the pass and the thrilling descent. A military checkpoint at South Pullu (4,663 metres; 15,300 feet) is a popular gathering point with cyclists, at the small roadside café backdropped by ragged rocks. It is hard surfaced at this point, but from South Pullu the road starts to fragment seriously. The Khardung La road sign is a blessed relief and signals the stopping point for local and international tourists, who pose for pictures while trying not to look queasy with a banging headache. At the very top, once you've done with kissing the ground, there's a souvenir shop that sells T-shirts that boast of your achievement. To help with the altitude sickness, a small canteen serves piping hot thukpa, maggi, chowmein and tea. It's not wise to hang around for too long at the top, so once your food has settled and you've swapped tales with the other cyclists, it's time to hurtle back down the pass for more scattering gravel – the anxiety over braking, steering and changing gears is palpable. Ride too fast and a skidding wheel will turn the exhilaration into terror in a split-second, so it pays to play it steady on the gradients here. The hairpin bends, crumbling road surface and dramatic drops flash before you as you give way to bigger, more powerful traffic. As they crunch their gears, and belch sooty smoke out into the air, it feels good to be alive in somewhere other than a comfort zone.

In the northernmost pocket of India, this old, precarious Himalayan pass has connected goat herders from Manali to Khardung La since earliest times. Though concentration prevents you from gazing lazily across the Zanskar Range, subconsciously you are aware of the stunning beauty of the Indus valley to the south-west. To the north-west, the Karakoram Range stands tall and foreboding: dark grey and draped with shawls of shimmering silver-white snow, set against a sky of brightest blue and glaciated valleys. Historically, the route was once a major caravan route from Leh to Kashgar in Central Asia as well as a Second World War supply road to China. Built over 100 years ago by the Indian Army, the road is only open during the summer months, yet even in this period it is prone to constant landslides and motor vehicle accidents.

Cyclists who attempt the Khardung La should be sure to wear layers of warm clothing, a pair of thermal gloves and thermal socks. They should also take preventative measures to lessen the effects of altitude sickness. Photo ID should be carried at all times (you'll need to present this at the military checkpoint). Don't forget your camera and some loose change for souvenirs and a hot snack (or tea) in the cafe. If you've previously suffered badly at high altitude, then consider the popular alternative option to minimise your exposure: doing the route to the summit by car with your bike and gear in the back, ready for the crossing and the descent on two wheels.

Endurance level: Difficult

Tip: Carry some essential pre-written questions in the local language as it is unlikely anyone you meet will speak anything other than their native tongue.

Contacts:
Indian Tourist Board
www.incredibleindia.org

Khardungla View Hotel
www.khardunglaview.com

YANGON–MANDALAY–MOUNT POPA, MYANMAR

In the words of Kipling, 'this is Burma and it is unlike any land you know about' – and, as Myanmar, Burma remains so today. Decades of international isolation have left this Southeast Asian country relatively untouched by the modern world and the local people are desperate for interaction. Culturally, it is fascinating and proud. Rural landscapes are untroubled by development. The abandoned temples and ancient palaces offer a faded grandeur. Intriguing and wholly unique, Myanmar begs exploration, from tribal villages and colourful floating markets to verdant valleys, gin-clear lakes and rolling central plains. I'm delighted to be cycling this mysterious nation with its robe-clad monks and roadside deities before the terrain, and its culture, changes beyond recognition.

My route runs from Yangon (Rangoon) to the expansive grasslands around Mandalay, before a thrilling descent from Mount Popa. Next, I plan to give my saddle a rest and take a river cruise along the Irrawaddy River to discover Inle Lake with its famous floating markets. Small settlements of bamboo huts and single-storey simple dwellings line the roadside, interspersed by farmland, fruit trees and forest. Women peer from windows, hens peck at grassy verges and piles of onions are sold out of sacks from front gardens.

Myanmar is a country that is gradually opening up, but visitors still face certain restrictions. Foreigners must stay at officially registered hotels and guesthouses, which means that inexpensive local guesthouses are generally off-limits. Camping is strictly forbidden, as is staying in the homes of local citizens. Do so and you're breaking the law and you'll be slapped with a hefty fine. Another constraint when mapping a Myanmar route as a visitor is that not all of the country is open to foreigners. However, routes are changing, with major link roads being reviewed, so it always pays to double check for an up-to-date list of navigable roads to avoid unwittingly wandering into a no-go zone.

Hospitality runs thick in Burmese blood, which means as a foreign visitor you'll be met with curious faces bearing beaming smiles everywhere you go. They are also a bicycle-loving nation – the roads are full of cycling vendors hawking grain, shrieking children pedalling off to school and workers heading off by bike to hoe the fields. Blissfully flat roads have helped popularise Myanmar as a destination with international leisure cyclists: conditions are relaxed and relatively easy. The challenge, however, is in the daily distances that need to be covered to get from one hotel to another – sometimes, it can be quite a slog (80–120 kilometres [50–75 miles] isn't uncommon).

Like much of South-east Asia, Myanmar's traffic rules are practically non-existent, so buzzing motorbikes, overloaded ox-drawn carts, rickshaws and wobbling cyclists compete

Photo: Ed Brambley

for road space in noisy chaos. Use a rugged touring bike or mountain bike to cope with the pot-holed roads – there are plenty of bike rental shops in Yangon and numerous specialist cycle tour companies serve this region too.

Crumbling colonial buildings stand in a dilapidated state in among Buddhist and Hindu monuments, churches and dome-roofed mosques. Take time to stroll through Little India and Chinatown in downtown Yangon, which is a frenzy of trading and eating activity with sizzling food stalls, curious street markets and vendor snack kiosks. Away from the main drag, roads are often dust-spewing rutted stretches of bare rock. Thankfully, once you've left the tooting horns and the automotive rumble of Yangon behind, Myanmar's quiet backroads offer a much less stressful pace. Stretches of country lanes offer total silence, apart from the sound of birdsong, with even the tiniest village, well off the tourist track, home to a gleaming golden temple and an army of saffron-robed monks. With mechanical farm equipment scarce, the fields are still worked by oxen and water buffalo, so the tranquillity is only broken by the occasional rattle of a generator-powered water pump.

Myanmar is safe (possibly the safest place on earth), so there is no fear in wandering aimlessly towards places as yet unknown. People are incredibly nice, friendly, helpful and genuinely warm. No places accept credit card, travellers cheques or ATM cards, so you need to arrive with cash. You need crisp, clean (perfect) US dollars because wrinkled or folded notes are instantly rejected – and it's non-negotiable. In most countries, foreigners carrying large amount of cash would immediately become a target, but not in Myanmar. So you can travel in comfortable assurance (assuming you've budgeted correctly). Basic rooms cost around $35 a night. Rooms are in short supply, so you will definitely need to book ahead. Internet access has opened up in Myanmar and you'll find free WiFi offered at many hotels and guest houses. Bring your mobile phone with you and buy a local sim card – it's invaluable when making hotel reservations in advance. Everybody wants your stay in Myanmar to be the best experience. They wave as you cycle by, shout 'hello' and try to help with restaurant recommendations. Water and food are easily available everywhere – both are cheap and plentiful. The biggest drain on your budget is accommodation, as demand for hotel rooms now outstrips supply. Hotel prices are on a continuing upward trajectory, with recent reports of per-night costs doubling.

At Inle Lake, visitors are encouraged to cycle along the eastern bank, where boat trips on the lake depart from a launch. You'll see Myanmar's famous leg-rowing fishermen out on the water and the communities living in stilt houses on the lake with their floating gardens, built up from strips of water hyacinth and mud and anchored to the bottom with bamboo poles. Then relish the ride around the lake itself to admire the views across waterlogged paddy fields.

To get up into the Western Shan Hills, it pays to get an early morning start for the long climb up to magnificent views. The town of Kalaw, a colonial-era British hill station, is home to some handsome buildings and was a favourite place for the British to settle because of the cool climate. Today, Kalaw is home to a diverse range of ethnicities, including those with Bangladesh ancestry, Pa Oh and Paluang hill tribes and the descendants of Nepalese Gurkhas who settled here. Plump fresh produce grows here in abundance and Kalaw, nestled among rolling hills, patchwork crops and grassy fields, has some fine kitchen-style restaurants in which regional specialities are served. From here to Ywar Ngan, there is an off-road ride through a seldom visited stretch where small communities of Pa Oh will watch curiously as you pedal by. Emerald pastures lead to dramatic limestone crags and lush flower gardens on a challenging, but rewarding ride, with plenty of fun downhill sections.

As the last royal capital of Myanmar, Mandalay was the first city to be ransacked by advancing British forces and is now a bustling commercial centre with colourful local markets. Some of the old architecture remains, though mainly in ruins. For one of the world's most jaw-dropping sunsets, pay a visit to Mandalay Hill – the colours that engulf the city sky are vibrant and intense.

Every cyclist who visits Mount Popa enjoys the pleasant ride through the dry zone on parched, tufted terrain that is markedly different from Myanmar's other regions. Slowly but surely, the road progresses to a rolling hill-climb with the ascents becoming more pronounced once you've left the last of the farmland behind. Suddenly, Mount Popa is there before you, with just a sharp, short ascent to the top. On the summit, find a beautiful resort with pool overlooking the Taung Kalat temple – a heavenly spot. Enjoy striking views across a colourful patchwork of farmland from bare soil fields ploughed by buffalo to swaying fields of corn.

Bagan is famous for its red-brick pagodas, which are best visited early in the morning as the arid sands of the Bagan plains are unbearably hot by the middle of the day. Many of the temples date back to the 14th and 19th centuries and the golden stupa of Shwezigon Pagoda provides a fine introduction to the region's rich history. Htilominlo Temple, nearby, is renowned for its grand plaster carvings, glazed sandstone and ornate and resplendent decor.

Endurance level: Moderate

Tip: Pack plenty of snacks and drinks as kiosks and shops are scarce in places.

Contacts:
Myanmar Cycle Tour
www.evaneos-travel.com

Burma By Bicycle
www.spiceroads.com

MEKONG RIVER, CAMBODIA

To Cambodians, the Mekong River is an intrinsic part of their character: a national lifeblood that runs deeps through the psyche of everyone in the countryside. Bank-to-bank river crossings ferry freshly hauled nets of fish, caught daily by local fishermen. Passing through the alluvial plain, the river nourishes paddy fields and upland crops to play a major role in Cambodian agriculture: feeding millions of people through the crops and a variety of fish it supports. Drinking, washing and irrigation are as important as the vital transport routes of the Mekong River for the many in riverside communities who live along its banks. Stretching a staggering 4,500 kilometres (2,796 miles) from the Tibetan Plateau to the South China Sea, the Mekong River Basin reaches through six South-east Asian countries. Through Cambodia, the river's average width is 1.5 kilometres (1 mile), crossing Stung Treng and Kratie Provinces in the upper part of the country, Kampong Cham Province and Phnom Penh Municipality, and flowing down towards Kandal Province to the South China Sea.

The riddle of cycling paths that run through the surrounding villages and countryside make the old French colonial city and fishing hub of Kratie a good base from which to explore by bike. Kratie town is famous for its wooden horse carts: a centuries-old tradition, it has been buoyed by a recently established local association of horse cart operators who conduct tours around the town and north along the Mekong River for visitors. Travelling by horse cart is a romantic way to experience the cobbled backstreets of Kratie and its many fine houses and statues. From here, adventurous cyclists will find it easy to journey for a few (or a few hundred) miles along the Mekong Discovery Trail, depending on the time you have available. The Mekong Discovery Trail is a network of safe, ecotourism journeys through some of the most natural and least populated sections of the Mekong River. It officially opened in 2008 to encourage the exploration of north-eastern Cambodia and its fishing culture. With its 1,200 species of fish, the river along the 180-kilometre Discovery Trail runs through areas particularly rich in flora and fauna. Cycling is a really effective way to get to the more remote stretches of the trail that have yet to be mapped in the densest forests on the river's banks.

A 80-kilometre (50-mile) stretch of the Mekong from Kratie will take around three days to complete at a leisurely pace and it is possible to rent bikes from CRDTours (part of the Cambodian Rural Development Team, which helps local communities supplement their fishing income with money from tourism). CRD also promotes conservation of the endangered Irrawaddy river dolphin, supplies detailed maps of the Mekong Discovery Trail and can help arrange private guides and home-stays for cyclists in several island communities. If you decide to hire bikes, bring helmets, panniers, clothing and bike repair kits – there are no cycle shops outside of Phnom Penh. Even daypacks are impossible to buy. The route shadows the Mekong as it flows through and around dense forests and islands, which form a sanctuary for numerous animal and plant species, especially birds. For some downtime out of the saddle, take a day trip down the river on a kayak to enjoy bird-watching, fishing or dolphin-spotting in deep, green pools. Around Kratie, the river also has rocky rapids that can be rafted with soft-shell turtles, giant catfish and thousands of fish species easily seen along quieter stretches.

The scenic islands of the Mekong are tucked among butterfly-scattered Ramsar wetlands and offer some resplendent sunset views against the silhouette of temples. Here, the lifestyles of the fishermen have changed little in centuries and you'll see sections of the river rarely travelled and very, very few tourists. Wispy smoke from floating kitchens means that meals of sticky rice (krolan) and pickled fish (nem) – two much-loved local dishes – are ready to taste. Maps also detail places where travellers can experience the authentic daily rituals of Khmer villages in a homestay. Owners often offer morning treks through forests that line the banks of the river out to the braided river channels and tallest, creeper-clad trees.

As a great trans-boundary river – and the world's twelfth-longest river – the Mekong boasts considerable seasonal variation in water level, resulting in rich and extensive mangroves and marshes. As it flows through China, Myanmar, Thailand, Lao PDR, Cambodia and Vietnam, the Mekong River Basin's biodiversity remains fundamental to the viability of the rural livelihoods of around 70 million people. Communities are learning to adapt, as have generations before them, as the impacts of climate change,

Photo: Helt

dam construction and deforestation bring changes to their lives. In the dry season, the river is an extraordinary maze of rocks, islets and sandbanks; in the cool season it has rock-pools that attract large numbers of migrating waterfowl and in the rainy season huge trees and massive roots emerge straight out of the fast flowing waters, eddies and whirlpools – an exhilarating spectacle. The best time to visit? Most cyclists choose to arrive in January and February to be certain that the monsoons have subsided and cycle trails are fully passable. Intrepid cyclists will find that many roads are in a bad condition after the wettest months – though there is usually a flat unpaved trail along the side that's perfect for bikes, if dry.

Be sure to learn the Cambodian greeting – the Sompiah – so that you can use it when introducing yourself. Confusingly, Cambodians have five different styles of greeting, depending on the age and status of the person. It involves placing their two palms together then bringing them close to their chest, before taking a bow. A blessing accompanies the act of Sompiah (Sur-s'dey) or a simple hello (Jum-reap sur) – it is generally done to those more senior, older or a higher rank as a mark of respect. The second step of the greeting is to place two palms together, your fingers under the lips – again, this is done as an act of respect to those we admire. During the Pol Pot era (1975–79), this greeting was lost. The third step applies to children to their family elders and the fourth step is for Buddhist monks and kings – monks are revered by everyone Cambodia-wide (even royalty will kneel to deliver Sompiah to a monk). The palms are pressed together with the fingers put to the eyebrow. The fifth step involves kneeling down before the Buddha statue in the temple, with the face low to the ground as Sompiah to the gods. Wherever or whoever you are, a Cambodian greeting is always accompanied by a broad, beaming smile. Slower gentler cycling speed allows for much more interaction with the locals: in the remotest Cambodian villages, you'll attract a huge amount of attention from cheering, flag-waving children and curious locals alike.

Endurance level: Moderate

Tip: Don't be shy to try the roadside street food – it's perfect for pepping up tired limbs and is tastier than it looks.

Contacts:
Tourism Cambodia
www.tourismcambodia.com

Cambodia Cycling
www.cambodiacycling.com

CAMERON HIGHLANDS, MALAYSIA

It has the clannish spirit of Scotland, a cool wet air that evokes the charm of the Welsh mountains and a panorama not unlike Sri Lanka's tea-growing regions. Yet, the lush greenery and soaring hills of the Cameron Highlands are in the north of Malaysia, rising up to and beyond 1,600 metres (5,249 feet) above sea level. Named after Sir William Cameron, a highly distinguished British commanding officer who first surveyed and mapped the area in 1885, the climate was popular with 19th-century British colonists because it felt like home. Today, many of the grand old buildings around Cameron Highlands originate from the colonial era, when the area was developed for cultivating tea.

To flourish, tea bushes require a considerable amount of moisture and were first grown on the slopes of the Cameron Highlands from seeds imported from China. They require 150–300 centimetres (59–118 inches) of rain, well distributed throughout the year, together with moisture drawn from heavy dew and morning fog, which is essential for the development of young leaves. Stagnant water, however, is injurious to roots, so they grow best on hill slopes where water drains away easily. A shade-loving plant, tea bushes sprout more bountifully when planted along with shady trees. Seeds are sown, and saplings are transplanted to a garden that is regularly hoed and weeded. Soils rich in humus and iron are considered to be the best soils for tea plantations, with relatively large proportions of phosphorus and potash the secret to the development of special flavours, as is the case in Darjeeling. Tea cultivation has become embedded in the local agricultural tradition and, since the late 1800s, tea plantations have dominated the scenery.

Though the hot, steamy gridlocked streets and modern skyscrapers of Kuala Lumpur are just 150 kilometres (93 miles) south, the metropolis feels like a world away. Not only is the temperature around 20°C less than the rest of Malaysia (bizarrely, you'll need a warm blanket at night and it's the only place in the country without air conditioning or ceiling fans), the character of the Cameron Highlands – with its market garden smallholdings, tea farms and vegetable fields – is utterly unique, yet you're a mere two hours away from the lowlands and sweat-dripping, tropical heat.

Be sure to take time out of the saddle to visit one of the many Orang Asli indigenous tribal villages in and around the Cameron Highlands on foot. These inhabitants of

Malaysia (Orange Asli means very broadly 'original people', 'natural people' or 'aboriginal people') still live in authentic community settings, set up high in strategic points along steep, hidden tracks. Leave your bike in the bushes (I marked mine with a flag made out of a t-shirt) and allow a guide to lead you up to the mud-and-thatch village. Several local tour guides offer a full-day package that includes tea-tasting at the BOH tea plantation, a visit to the spectacular Mossy Forest (or Cloud Forest) when, in rising fast temperatures, it's possible to witness a soft, all-encompassing magical white mist descend – truly beautiful, eerie and mysterious – set against the deep, green moss and delicate milky-white orchids. It feels like you've stepped into Middle Earth.

With four possible approach routes to the Cameron Highlands by bike, it's important to weigh up the different cycling experiences and scenery each offers. The most well-frequented is the road from Tapah – if you're coming from the main Kuala Lumpur to Ipoh road, this is the default route. It's a nice ride, though busy at the weekends with holiday traffic. It has a 40-kilometre rise at a fairly gradual 3–4 per cent, mostly shaded, with a popular waterfall stop in the middle where you can grab some fruit, drinks or a meal. It'll bring you up to the main Cameron plateau at Ringlet. If you keep going, you'll get another nice twelve kilometres (seven and a half miles) of climbing at some much meatier gradients up to Tanah Rata.

I discounted the well-frequented, fast dual-carriageway route up from Ipoh because I didn't want to sprint straight there – even though it offers cyclists a joyously arduous eight-kilometre (five-mile) climb, a lot of it between 9 and 12 per cent, up to Brinchang at 1,600 metres (5,249 feet) before heading down through the town and on to Tanah Rata. I chose, instead, the road from Sungai Koyan, which

Photo: Will Ellis

is absolutely desolate and therefore wonderfully peaceful, climbing steadily for the 100 kilometres (62 miles) through amazing scenery. I left at daybreak because it is quite exposed and doesn't offer a lot of shade.

Next time, I have vowed to take the most challenging route from Gua Musang, which climbs more than 3,000 metres (9,843 feet) before it spits you out in Brinchang 120 kilometres (75 miles) after a string of lung-bursting gradients at a whopping 10–12 per cent.

Whichever approach you choose, the great news is that the Cameron Highlands has everything a cyclist desires: hotels with perfect beds for resting tired limbs, a superb range of decent restaurants (at every budget point), several spas that offer a menu of sports massages and plenty of shops to stock up on bottled water, snacks, sun cream and get bike repairs done. Bring a camera because you may see monkeys, wild boar and, with luck, an elephant en route. Pack a tent for overnight flexibility (the rain and mists can sometimes play havoc with a riding schedule) and bring warm and waterproof clothing just in case. Passing trucks will often stop and offer cyclists a lift in the event of a sudden change in weather; rainstorms can mean it is too wet and dark to continue on two-wheels safely. Another tip is water: don't worry too much if you run out on the way because there are plenty of small streams and springs by the side of the road where you can cool down and refill your bottles. Some of the farmsteads will have tables outside piled high with strawberries, corn, cabbage and all kinds of other freshly grown goodies.

Endurance level: Moderate–Difficult

Tip: Early morning start? You'll need thermal clothing or warm layers – it's chillier that it looks.

Contacts:
Cameron Highlands Tourism
www.cameronhighlands.com

Cameron Highlands Travel Guide
www.cameronhighlandsinfo.com

Tourism Malaysia
www.tourism.gov.my

FANGYUAN TO TAITUNG, TAIWAN

The island of Taiwan, just off the south-east coast of China, may not be that well known as a bike touring destination, but this isn't for lack of two-wheeled thrills. Numerous mountains in this 35,980-square-kilometre landscape offer plenty of thigh-busting challenges, while a sub-tropical temperature ensures a pleasing cycling climate. More than a hundred peaks top 3,000 metres (9,843 feet), with Jade Mountain (Yu Shan) just shy of 4,000 metres (13,123 feet). Undeveloped tourism potential means that Taiwan remains largely ignored by foreign visitors, so all the prime cycling routes are free from touring bikes. The roads are pretty good, better than you'd imagine: the beautiful scenery more than makes up for the occasional pothole and crumbling asphalt. To travel the narrow lanes of the East Coast with its pretty fishing villages is an absolute labour of love.

On arrival in Taiwan, Canadians, Americans and people from most European nations receive a one-month visa, so the red-tape is minimal for a 30-day cycle tour. Once the airport staff realise you plan to cycle to Taitung, they may well pass on names and addresses of people they know en route to stay with, eat with or visit. They may even pass on a tip that Taiwan police stations double as cyclist pit stops – and as strange as it sounds, it's actually true. This can be especially useful to know if you're chased by a dozen or so angry stray dogs, suffer recurring punctures or simply need somewhere to escape the midday sun. They also offer free water and lend tools and a helping hand to change a tyre: reassuring news.

Crossing the island by bike from West to East takes you on a stunning journey through a heavenly landscape of dramatic peaks and gorges with divine views. At times, the Pacific Ocean stretches for miles and miles beyond a terrace of verdant green rice paddies. It is hard to feel the intensity of an epic hill-climb when the surrounding countryside is such a distraction. Highway 17 snakes long the coast, then Highway 9 cuts through the magnificent East Rift Valley. Both require stamina (some hills seem to stretch on for ages), but to reach the summit, sweat-drenched and praying for an easy few miles, you're always rewarded with spectacular bird's-eye views before an epic downhill coasting. For a mid-route treat, be sure to make time to visit the Japanese-style hot springs at Ruisui. – The geo-thermal bubbles help to soothe cycle-weary limbs and you can stay overnight.

Taitung is a great place from which to enjoy an island excursion with Orchid Island (Lanyu) a Taiwanese secret well worth discovering, especially if your thighs are on fire. Set aside a couple of days to explore this 46-square-kilometre beach idyll, characterised by typhoon-carved rock formations of bizarre shapes and sizes. Catch a ferry from Taitung (expect a choppy crossing) and prepare to be seduced by simple island life.

Orchid Island is home to the indigenous Yami, who sell traditional crafts and eke out a living fishing from wooden canoes, as they have done for almost a millennium. The Yami are the only maritime ethnic people among Taiwan's Austronesian cultures and call themselves Tao (meaning 'people on the island'). During the 50 years of Japanese colonial rule, in 1895 the government declared Orchid Island a research zone and prohibited outsiders from entering or cultivating land there, which helped preserve the traditional lifestyle and culture on the island. This ancient volcanic island, with a 45-kilometre coastal road, is shaped by nine mountains: the highest, Hongtou Mountain (Red Head Mountain), is 548 metres (1,798 feet) above sea level. Sunrise transforms this towering peak with a mesmerising red glow, hence the name. Rocks, steep mountains, rivers and beaches are the main topographical features of the island. Every crevice, every nook, every twisted and gnarled rock has been shaped by the wind, rain and maritime weather.

The Yami feel their island is bonded to the sea and that they are bonded to each other: couples marry for life and work hard to achieve their goals. As a fishing-dependent culture, men team up with boats to strengthen their economic might in a paternal society. They operate a share system that is rooted in the life and rituals on Orchid Island: a natural result of the 'mutually beneficial' interpersonal relations of the Yami people. Without a well-developed religion, they fear evil spirits and pray to the sun or the moon. Their calendar corresponds to the flying fish season and is wholly connected to marine life and the movements of ocean currents. From February to October, work is assigned to the fishing, preparation, distribution and storage of flying fish and these close ties to the ocean are central to ceremonies and rituals. Owning a boat means

Photo: Eric Deng

owning the ocean in Yami culture and the Boat Launching Ceremony is a key ritual.

Named after the delicate *Phalaenopsis* orchids, a very rare species that once flourished in abundance on the island, Orchid Island is cultivated for taro, sweet potatoes, yams and millet – Yami food staples. Rice, introduced by the Chinese in recent times, accompanies centuries-old seafood recipes. Deep-blue waters boast some of the most incredible snorkelling with coral gardens in brilliant rainbow hues that say 'dive right in'. Palm-topped beach bars bid cyclists a warm welcome – an ice-cold Taiwanese Gold Medal beer truly hits the spot after a hard day in the saddle. Local accommodation is basic, either a family-run B&B or a rustic homestay; but with soft sand and glistening blue waters, a few days of swimming and fishing is utter bliss. The Yami are also keen to inform foreign visitors about Taiwanese aboriginal culture and will be gape-mouthed at a Lycra-wearing cyclist.

Back on the mainland, choose the small, little-used roads through beautiful scenery that characterise Taiwan's narrow eastern coastal belt – you'll need to stray onto a few unavoidable stretches of busier, bigger roads, but these often have designated cycle lanes. The terrain varies from gently undulating along parts of the east coast to steep ascents and descents over the coastal mountain range.

Visiting Taiwan in autumn (October to December) offers cyclists clear, warm and sunny weather (18–28°C) as does spring (March to May). Summers (mid-May to the end of September) are hot and humid (28–35°C) with the risk of heavy tropical downpours and typhoons. If you are used to the heat and don't mind cycling through an occasional heavy shower, you'll enjoy riding through lush green hills in the summer months when the countryside is alive with vivid blooms, fruits and wildlife.

Endurance level: Moderate

Tip: Be prepared for frequent use of the horn in and around built-up areas – drivers seem to toot and honk at random. Loudly.

Contacts:
Taiwan Tourism
eng.taiwan.net.tw

Government of Taiwan
www.taiwan.gov.tw

QINGHAI LAKE, CHINA

China has a unique, special relationship with the bicycle. Before it became the economic powerhouse it is today, and nobody had the means to afford vehicular transport, Chinese society cycled – everywhere. Factory operatives to work; teachers to school; lawyers to court; commuters into the city. Food was delivered by bicycle (often still alive and breathing). 1949 was a turning point for Chinese-made cycles: the bike was promoted by The Party as the 'people's vehicle' and production on a massive scale ensued. Bicycles were endorsed by city planners and over a million were made in one year alone. Cycles were as essential as rice: an efficient and egalitarian necessity. Great swarms of thousands of cyclists surged along broad four-lane roads, gripping the handlebars in equality and comradeship.

China was the undisputed capital of the bicycle world

Photo: Charlie Fong

and outside of the main cities it still is. The car was easily integrated into Shanghai, Beijing and the affluent Chinese urban sprawl in the 1980s, yet the cycle is still a king. In recent years, China has put enormous effort into trying to encourage its population to re-embrace the bicycle in a bid to reduce air pollution and traffic jams. Today the country has become a leader in sharable biking with its fleet of 650,000 public bikes. The world's top four bike-share cities are all in China. Almost 60 per cent of all bicycles sold around the world are Chinese made. As a nation, China's relationship with and perception of cycling has changed dramatically over the years: first, a cultural icon, then a sign of backwardness. And now, well it's Amsterdam-style cool.

Since 2011, possibly prompted by 100-kilometre (62-mile), nine-day traffic jams and health-damaging air quality, Chinese citizens have been tempted back in the saddle through bike share programmes. No longer seen as purely utilitarian, cycling is now part of a hipster bike culture popular with younger Chinese. Together with the ever-expanding ring roads encircling the cities, the bicycle paths are now being beautifully maintained for the expanding middle class. Cycling enthusiasts have helped to revitalise the image of the bicycle: it's no longer a symbol of poverty but a status symbol. Can you still find the ubiquitous dark-green Flying Pigeon bike of the past?

Yes, but most have had funky modern paint-jobs. Bikes have become a form of identity expression. Today you'll find day-glow bikes with customised features, graffiti-sprayed or pimped-up with glitter and bling. To see a fascinating variety of these deeply individualised bikes, head to any section of Qinghai Lake in the Tibetan area – a 360-kilometre (224-mile) route in total that is home to the Qinghai Lake International Cycling Race each July. Here, the slick, asphalt cycle path is a cycling paradise: a perfectly manicured surface as smooth as the finest marble.

Running from Qinghai to Heimahe Town, Gangcha County, Xihai Town and Huangyuan County at 3,200 metres (1,988 feet) above sea level, this high-altitude route attracts flashy, kooky and oh-so-cool customised cycles in a range of stylish, bespoke designs. Ride-wear is equally individual and designed to cope with the area's day-and-night temperature variations (20°C versus 10°C in August) and sun-protection measures. Though Qinghai Lake is a sacred lake of the Tibetan people, cyclists are encouraged to enjoy the ever-changing colours of the saline waters from their saddle. The hues of the water alter according to different viewing angles, time of day and season, and attract huge flocks of birds that, combined, rival the rainbow of colours of the cyclists, their bikes and cycling gear.

As Western China's largest body of water, Qinghai Lake spans 4,635 square kilometres (2,880 square miles) and is famous for its islands and spectacular high-mountain scenery. The region is also home to a rich cultural mix of Tibetan, Mongolian and Muslim communities, as well as a growing cycling fraternity. Once the lake has thawed from the bitterly cold icy freeze of the winter months, the greenery flourishes and the flowers bloom. Reaching a depth of nineteen metres (62 feet), the lake has many species of fish, despite being almost twice as salty as seawater. Cyclists enjoy the companionship of other cycle nuts, or enjoy the solitude that the Qinghai Province offers as the least populated area of China. The lake, located far away from major towns, is fertile, pure and clear and well-served by cycle-friendly hotels and campgrounds.

The Qinghai Bike Race takes place to coincide with the Tour de France and brings in thousands of cyclists to this favourite biking route. Big pale-yellow sand dunes and sparkling ponds are just a part of the beautiful bird-scattered scenery, with Bird Island an important site for thousands of exotic migratory birds in the north-west corner of the lake – a magical and magnificent birders dream. The rigours of the altitude can make the lake a tough challenge, even for serious cyclists, so it is advisable to arrive in plenty of time to acclimatise properly. China's most resplendent, natural scenery is the reward for your trouble, running right along the cycle path: a lush deep-green prairie the colour of emerald dotted with yellow-and-white wildflowers. Snowy mountain peaks in the distance are topped by drifting marshmallow clouds and silhouetted by bright, golden sunlight. It is this gorgeous countryside and pure mountain air that lures cyclists from around Asia and beyond.

As the fountainhead of China's three greatest rivers – the Yangtze, the Yellow and the Lantsand – the well-nourished Qinghai region is revered as the 'water tower of the nation' and has been populated since the Palaeolithic period, attractive to nomadic tribes for its bountiful water and grassy plains. Historic relics and archaeological sites are plentiful, reflecting the cultures and ancestry of Qinghai Province, from the 14th-century Dongguan Giant Mosque, one of the largest Islamic places of worship in China, to the Buddhist Longwu Temple in Tongren and the Kumbum Monastery in Xining. Several long-distance buses take cycles and depart from the transit station in Xining for the town of Heimahe on the lake's south-west corner. The journey takes five hours and stops at other towns around the lake if Heimahe isn't your final destination.

Endurance level: Moderate

Tip: Public toilets can be hygienically poor and it can be nicer to answer a call of nature in the leafy privacy of the great outdoors.

Contacts:
China National Tourist Office
www.cnto.org

Cycling China
www.china.org.cn

HIROSHIMA, JAPAN

Lying in the south-west of Japan's main island, Honshu, the Hiroshima area is wedged between the picturesque Chūgoku Mountains and Seto Inland Sea. Though its name will long be synonymous with deadly A-bomb blasts, Hiroshima has become a byword for awesome cycling with two-wheeled adventurers across the world in recent years. A single, 65-kilometre (40-mile) route between an interconnected series of Japanese islands is shared like a military secret between the foot soldiers on cycling forums, where much is made of marble-smooth route that stretches across mighty suspension bridges offering gasp-inducing ocean views. Flags dot the way, to publicise the region's cycling mass participation event: Cycling Shimanami – an opportunity for more than 6,000 cyclists to speed along a choice of distances, from a simple fifteen-kilometre sprint to a full 110 kilometres (68 miles) up-and-back.

Japan is renowned for its refined hospitality (omotenashi) and even the most gruelling cycling itinerary, formed of a quick turnaround between each stop, allows for a steady average of 35 kilometres a day – so it is rare to spend more than five hours in Lycra on any one day. The comfy pace ensures you can pay an impromptu visit to Shinto temples, rice wine distilleries, bonsai gardens and a host of cultural relics you pass along the way. It is here that you can see gorgeous cherry blossom in spring or golden leaves in autumn. Yet nothing can prepare you for the far reach of the world's longest series of suspension bridges – the Shimanami Kaido Highway.

Start from the old port town of Mitarai with its boatyards and follow the Shimanami Kaido Highway as it slinks from island to island in Japan's Inland Sea. Linking Imabari in Shikoku with the Hiroshima Prefecture, this bicycle-friendly 70-kilometre (44-mile) route stretches across six islands of outstanding natural beauty. Spanning the vast stretches of sea for as far as the eye can see, these immense towering structures vary in size, with the longest, the four-kilometre (two-and-a-half-mile) Kurushima-Kaikyō Bridge, a truly stunning triple-spanning arc of sensuous curves. Magnificent in stature and design, the Shimanami Kaido Highway initially skirts a densely forested slope before sweeping over the mammoth elevated stretches. From the thick foliage of the wilderness roads, the raised freeway offers lofty views of wide open water across oyster beds and golden sunny skies. Each beautifully curved slim section of bridge is suspended with a spaghetti of wires and it gracefully straddles the islands. A blue line denotes the cycleway so that you know you're travelling safely in the bike zone: no need to juggle an unfurled map or worry about the muddle of roads leading off each junction, which makes island navigation a breeze.

Another comfort on the Shimanami Kaido Highway is the company you'll keep – you'll encounter dozens of fellow cyclists, from road racers to elderly men and women on town bikes and each is treated with courtesy by car drivers, who pass slowly and sedately with no inkling of impatience. No close shaves, no being forced into the curb. In Japan, drivers leave enough room between them and a bike frame for a double-decker bus to nip through.

At the midway point, where the Shimanami Cycleway leads to local backroads of Innoshima Island, the route becomes an off-the-beaten-track affair: bumpy in places, eroded in patches, and weaving through small fishing villages and market garden settlements set right on the roadside. Around each and every turn, the route ventures into a different cluster of houses or smallholding buildings. Apart from the short climbs, the going is predominantly flat, until it starts to cut back towards the coast with lots of shady spots for off-the-bike rest stops in peaceful tranquillity.

If you can, book a room at the Onomichi U2 Hotel Cycle: a custard-coloured former warehouse carefully re-modelled to cater specifically for cyclists. Conveniently located at the start of the Shimanami Cycleway, this hotel has a coffee shop, restaurant and bike repair centre, and is decorated with an assortment of bicycling paraphernalia. Order a plate of okonomiyaki (noodles and cabbage) and a sake if you dare. Bicycle hire is around 500 yen a day (plus a refundable 1,000 yen as a deposit) and there are always plenty of cyclists there with tips to swap regarding the photogenic scenery, a favourite pitstop and potential nuisances.

If you have time, pay a visit to the A-Bomb Dome, which many people will recognise from photographs. Designed in 1915 by a Czech architect as a symbol of peace, the building was partially damaged by the atomic bomb, but remained standing, and is now designated a UNESCO World Heritage Site. Today, it is a focal point for people's prayers for a lasting peace, together with the Hiroshima Peace Memorial Park

Photo: clear_and_sunny

located at the centre of Hiroshima City. Now a blossom-filled gathering point featuring well over 300 cherry trees, picnics and river cruises on the nearby Motoyasu River offer wonderful views in spring. It is here, too, in August each year, that the Hiroshima Peace Memorial Ceremony takes place, during which a one-minute silence is observed for the victims at 8.15am, the time of the explosion. In the evening, small lanterns are lit and floated downstream carrying messages to console the souls of the dead. It is a spellbinding sight: hundreds of flickering lanterns bobbing on the waters of the Motoyasu under a moonlit sky.

In a fine example of expert Japanese planning, there are bicycle rental shops and drop-off points on pretty much every island. This means, should you decide to cut your journey short, there is always somewhere close at hand to leave the bike. All along the routes served by the long-reach of the Shimanami Kaido Highway, you'll find cycle-friendly places to stop and grab something to eat and drink. If you can, pre-book your bike rental before you arrive and on an exact model so that you don't simply get handed one that has been rejected by everyone else – or worse, a bike that has been recovered after being abandoned in a poor state by the side of the road.

Endurance level: Moderate–Difficult

Tip: Keen to camp? You'll be considered eccentric and an oddball, so expect the locals to attempt to coax you to the local hotel.

Contacts:
Cycling Japan
www.cyclingjapan.jp

Hiroshima Cycle Tours
www.cyclekyoto.com

Hiroshima Tourism
www.visithiroshima.net

AUSTRALASIA

MUNDA BIDDI, AUSTRALIA

Slicing through miles of thick eucalyptus trees and native bush that are home to western brush wallaby, western grey kangaroos and brush-tail possum, the Munda Biddi (which means path through the forest in the Noongar Aboriginal language) cycle trail runs from Mundaring, a suburb located 34 kilometres (21 miles) east of Perth on the Great Eastern Highway, to Albany, a port city in the Great Southern region of Western Australia – the longest track of its kind in the world. Built through a stunning undeveloped natural corridor, this world-class nature trail contains some of Australia's finest unspoiled forest in year-round cycling weather. There are few places left in the world where a 1,000-kilometre (621-mile) trail could be blessed by year-round cycling weather and plants and wildlife not found anywhere else in the world. Little wonder the Munda Biddi Trail is on a zillion cyclists' bucket list, with its gentle slopes and well-maintained dirt tracks suitable for all cycling abilities and paces.

With its vast empty expanses and never-ending roads, Australia has the perfect landscape for epic journeys and long-distance challenges. Blood-red sands, craggy peaks, brown deserts and golden sands vie for position with winelands, rainforests, ravines and a thousand pretty isles. The tangled bush of the outback, with its hot-and-dusty off-road cycle trails and far-reaching tracks, cuts through deserts, rainforest and swampland.

In among this, you'll find the famous Munda Biddi Trail: a wilderness route conceived by the West Australian Mountain Bike Association (WAMBA). This small, motivated group of passionate off-road cyclists sought funding to develop a 'sustainable, world-class, long distance off-road cycle trail that showcases the unique natural and cultural features of the state's south-west, while enhancing the quality of life for all Western Australians and the visitors it attracts'. It has more than exceeded this goal. Construction on the resplendent Munda Biddi Trail began in 2001 and, thanks to the incredible efforts of dedicated volunteers, it reached half-way seven years later in 2008. In 2013, the trail was ready for the first cyclists prepared to complete the inaugural end-to-end ride. Today, more than 21,000 visitors from all over the world arrive at the Munda Biddi Trail with their bicycle clips at the ready. Few purpose-built cycle paths boast such a jaw-dropping setting through dark knotted forests, fragrant woodlands and coastal plains flanked by cliff-tops, inter-tidal waters and saline lagoons. Jarrah forests (the local name for eucalyptus) contain bountiful plants, including low-lying scrub and giant bushes scattered with flowers that are home to a wide diversity of mammals, amphibians, reptiles and birds. Whirring gears often cause feathers to flutter or balls of fur to scuttle and scurry in zig-zags across the track.

Granite outcrops characterise the roads that are flanked by one of Western Australia's most common bushland shrubs, prickly moses, which forms a feathery custard-coloured carpet beside the trail. Gorgeous splashes of pastel peek out from towering feathery ferns to betray the presence of velvety orchids in yellow, white or pink. Tall grass trees abound, attracting swarms of bees when they flower, while birds flit along from bush to bush in search of water and food. Almost all of the towns along the way – including Mundaring, Jarrahdale, Dwellingup, Collie, Boyanup, Donnybrook, Jarrahwood, Nannup, Donnelly River Village, Manjimup, Quinninup, Pemberton, Northcliffe, Walpole, Denmark and Albany – have great cycle supply shops, grocery stores and places to stock up on water and snacks.

In among it all, the broad girth of the mighty Murray River is visible beyond paperbark (melaleuca) thickets and flooded gum woodlands. Further south toward Collie, the vegetation consists chiefly of paperbarks and flooded gums, and as the trail streaks through sand-flats, banksia and grass trees shelter a scattergun of small lizards. The section from Collie to Jarrahdale has a mixture of deforested areas and stands of virgin trees that were rooted in Western Australia's ancient forests before the arrival of European settlers and their axes. A spaghetti of mud-bank creeks crisscross the area and play a vital role in nourishing vast meadows of wild flowers as well as the sprouting soap bush and rushes along creek beds. On the approach to Jarrahdale, cyclists have the thrill of passing through a stand of white gum trees: soaring up to 25 metres (82 feet) in height with pinkish-brown trunks, they are commonly found in broad shallow valleys or on low ridges. Here, the entire forest floor and its fertile leaf litter is a home to small mammals, birds, reptiles and whining insects. Donnelly River Village, once a lumber town that buzzed to the sound of saw mills, is a weekend vacation destination with its fields of semi-tame kangaroos and emus. Look out for pretty blue wrens around here – and listen

Photo: Murray Foubister

out too for the distinctive tripled-noted call of the flocks of native Australian ringneck parrots: a gregarious green bird with a red front band and a yellow 'ringneck' hind collar that nests in the rooftops.

Heading south towards Pemberton, you will cycle through some beautiful areas of blackbutt (yarri), as the trail initially follows the Donnelly River along narrow trails bordered with soapbush. Be prepared for a riot of colour if you journey the trail during spring because the area is blessed with vast carpets of wildflowers and magnificent karri trees which begin to dominate the forest.

Closer to Northcliffe cyclists will find an abundance of wildflowers in the spring. The forest is generally damper, with associated plant life, such as ferns, abundant and the presence of water along most of the route also means the bird life is prolific. Quokkas, small marsupials found mainly on Rottnest Island near Perth, but once widespread on the mainland before the introduction of foxes, have been spotted along this section and their numbers are increasing through Operation Fox Glove.

Between Northcliffe and Walpole spans a long section of almost 130 kilometres (426 miles) with terrain varying from karri forest to swampland, coastal dunes, beaches and back to the forest, this time to the mighty tingle trees.

In the South, the Trail passes through stands of karri, Warren River cedar and sheoak trees and across granite mounds, before reaching the dunes and sand ridges with their mix of peppermint and banksia scrub.

Many cyclists adore the wild south coast section of the Munda Biddi Trail because of the incredible variation of flora and fauna they see along the way, from the rare and elusive ground parrot to western tiger snakes. Cycling through the coastal heathlands is pure bliss on a sunny morning as you prepare for arrival in Albany – the southern terminus of the Munda Biddi Trail. In each settlement you pass, you can camp under canvas or overnight in a quaint B&B or Aboriginal family homestay. Doing the 1,000 kilometres (621 miles; or part of it) comes with a myriad of options: join a group tour or do it the independent way on a self-guided cycling tour with a tent and a B&B handbook. To cycle the trail end-to-end takes between two and four weeks (at least 100 people each year become 'End-to-enders' by completing the entire trail). You can dip in and out of the trail as it can be entered via lots of different access points with plenty of towns and villages nearby. This is a really flexible option that encourages cyclists to tailor their experience to the time of year, the section ridden and the age group, and their fitness and experience. However you cycle the landscape, the trail is utterly engrossing – the tranquil atmosphere and the constant interaction with wildlife gives you a privileged connection with nature and your bike.

Cyclists should be sure to pick up a relevant Munda Biddi map and gather as much local information before starting off: trail surfaces vary so it is important to be sensible about the speed you'll be able to clock-up on unsealed, bumpy bike paths. Roughly speaking, the trail is split into sections of between 30 and 40 kilometres (eighteen and 25 miles; some as low as nine kilometres [five and a half miles] and as high as 55 kilometres [34 miles]) with a campsite or hut at each point. The sections fall into eight bigger regional splits and an online calculator has been designed to help with route planning – it includes all campsites, towns, recreation sites and legal vehicle access points on the Munda Biddi Trail maps. On the trail itself, there are two types of marker: those located on yellow posts and others on trees. Located every few hundred metres or so, the markers also denote critical intersections and point to the next section. The campsites are purpose-built, cycle-friendly and, best of all, entirely free! All you will need to bring is some toilet paper (for the composting toilet). Water is available (use sparingly and treat the water before drinking) and there are picnic tables, undercover bike storage, a sleeping shelter for approximately 25 people on four timber platforms and cleared tent sites. No open fires are permitted, only designated fuel stoves. You'll also need a warm sleeping bag and clothing for cool evenings. Campsites marked with a red car on the map have vehicular access. Other private campgrounds are located near to the trail, but fees apply for most of them.

Keen to take your time? Then be sure to pay a visit to as many of the towns you pass by: each one has its own unique character and through-riders generally stay at least one or two nights to do their washing, buy supplies and taste some of the region's delectable wines. Cycling hopheads can also indulge their beer obsession along the Munda Biddi Trail with one of Western Australia's tempting craft beers – or two.

Endurance level: Easy–Moderate

Tip: Keep a spare lip balm at hand to daub on saddle-sores to help them heal after slogging along this sweaty, rugged route.

Contacts:
The Munda Biddi Trail
www.mundabiddi.org.au

Visit Western Australia
www.westernaustralia.com

HOBART–STRAHAN–LAUNCESTON, TASMANIA

It was a seductive proposition: a chance to explore the unworldly terrain of a wave-carved atoll blessed with old-growth eucalyptus and golden button-grass moorlands. I'd be traversing a land packed with hundreds of miles of dolerite cliffs, root-riddled emerald forests and glacial valleys virtually untroubled since the last ice age. The catch was I'd be on a bike, but that just intrigued me more. And so it came to be that I arrived in the Southern Hemisphere with cycle clips at the ready.

In his memoir of a Tasmanian childhood, Peter Conrad wrote: 'We were an offshore island off the shore of an offshore continent, victims of a twofold alienation'. Certainly, Tasmania's twelve-millennia split from the Australian mainland earned it a far-flung remoteness, befitting one of last feral wildernesses on earth. Tasmania's mystical geological attributes have been fiercely defended by a decades-long conservation struggle. The result is an eye-popping ecosystem of untamed moss-clad woodlands, soaring ferns and an oddball assortment of bizarre creatures. Much of the island is protected with the Tasmanian Wilderness World Heritage Area recognised by UNESCO in 1982 for its outstanding natural and cultural value. Today, to travel Tasmania is to experience a triumph of Mother Nature and her jewel-box of natural treasures. Fittingly, the island's tourist trade values its unique environment, so in crowd-free Tasmania a bicycle is the perfect way to travel. No roar of traffic. No vehicles to force me into the gutter. No spewing diesel fumes.

My journey begins in Hobart, where the glorious sunshine I had pre-ordered arrives on cue. It's hot; in fact, it's positively steamy and not at all what I'd expected from Australia's most rain-drenched state. At 7am the road is already a blurry haze as I stroll around Tasmania's capital; a fine deepwater port centred on Sullivans Cove at the base of brooding Mount Wellington. A neat city of clapboard houses and Georgian sandstone buildings, Hobart is Australia's second-oldest urban settlement; a handsome town dotted with statues of British dignitaries gazing far out to sea. In modern times a funky-chic waterfront quarter has joined the city's colonial core, adding lovingly restored warehouse bars and floating restaurants to Hobart's architectural and spiritual mix.

At roughly the same size as Switzerland, Tasmania offers plenty of cycling possibilities, and I have chosen to journey the island's rugged western coast. I'll be in the saddle for a week covering around 72–80 kilometres (45–50 miles) a day – hardly the Tour de France, but a testing schedule none the less. I unfurl a map and brace myself for the physical challenge ahead. With panniers secured and sprockets, valves and spokes double-checked, I hit the inner city Cycleway with a wobble. Launceston here I come!

Thankfully, the 80-kilometre (50-mile) route north-west from Hobart to the sleepy town of Hamilton is awash with colour; a boon for cyclists like me who need constant visual stimulation to dull the ache of tired limbs. From Hobart's Cenotaph area, the Cycleway runs along an old railway line next to the water in a beautiful, sleek paved stretch. Then the countryside takes over to offer yellow-green pasture littered with sweet-smelling wildflowers. Squiggly S-shaped creeks and lush valleys grab my attention en route to New Norfolk, then oast houses and hop fields remind me of southern England in Bushy Park. Parts of me are sore and chafed, but I make it in one piece to sleepy Hamilton, a charming limestone settlement seemingly lost in time. Blessed with

1830s faded good looks, the town was built by convict labourers. Today it makes an excellent base from which to trek the leafy trails of Mount Field National Park.

First-time cyclists in Tasmania will find the roads refreshingly free of congestion with smooth-paved routes devoid of potholes, lumps and bumps. After a day of relaxing into the swing of things, I feel wholly in-tune with Mother Nature. Now, rather than fretting about my mile-rate, I gaily abandon myself to the landscape. My syncopated pounding on the pedals produces a comforting rhythmic pulse as one beautiful village leads to another. I'm soon mesmerised by a heady scenic blur, while the miles – and days – slip effortlessly by.

Continuing north from Hamilton, I set my sights on Tarraleah and earmark Ouse for a pit-stop along the way. A strong Scots heritage prevails in the aptly named Central Highlands and mist-shrouded Ouse has a Brigadoon-style feel to it, set among wind-swept trees and hardy scrub. A handful of residents live in a scattering of slatted wooden homes surrounded by tufted tussocks on blood-red soil. My calves begin to slow-burn after a rigorous gradual incline and as I ease up by an inky-green river rich in trout, I wish I had a Band Aid for a badly blistered toe.

A fatigue-beating bar of homespun Cadbury's provides a burst of energy as I criss-cross streams and bush-land along a secluded, peaceful expanse. Free from the hubbub of noise pollution, I imbibe the luxury of silence and, a little tipsy on tranquillity, revel in the only audible sound – my own breath. It's a strangely spiritual experience and I feel humbled by my environment: no wonder the Tasmanian wilderness is often described as 'the elixir of our souls'. At Tarraleah, I dump my bike at the farmhouse B&B and enjoy a leisurely stroll. Flocks of little songbirds dart from skinny copses, while eagles circle scouring the ground for prey. After a

Photo: JJ Harrison

robust meal of fish pie and some fine Tasmanian pinot gris, I fall into a deep slumber with thoughts of another tarmac mystery tour fuelled by the purest air in the world.

Fortified by a mile-high pile of pancakes, I survive the series of gruelling hills out of Tarraleah and recover my composure just in time to enjoy the thrills of a rapid descent from Mount Arrowsmith. A succession of ups-and-downs deposits me at the old mining district on the slopes of Mount Owen, where I face the final muscle-pounding ascent of the day. The upside is a white-knuckle six-and-a-half-kilometre (four-mile) downhill blood-pumper into Queenstown, along a winding lunar moonscape in which there are 99 terrifying bends. Sensibly, I opt to complete the remaining 48 kilometres (30 miles) to Strahan by steam train and with my bike safely stored in the guard's van, I make the most of the $99 ticket, whooping with joy at monster-sized ferns in a zillion hues of green.

Before breakfast, I pottered around Strahan's pretty harbour to snap up a few oyster-shell souvenirs. After a downhill chase from Mount Murchison, I sprinted into the village of Tullah, where I hopped aboard a shuttle bus to spare my battered limbs. Cradle Mountain's jagged contours form the northern end of a spectacular national park, Lake St Clair, where fearsome dolerite peaks, dense rainforest and varicoloured beech trees are riddled by icy streams. Dozens of hidden trails offer hikes of every dimension, from ten-minute genteel wanders to full-day arduous stomps. The view across Dove Lake to Cradle Mountain is a genuine not-to-be-missed highlight with the Dove Lake Loop Track an excellent trek through stunning cool temperate rainforest against steep mountain slopes. The famous Overland Track also begins from here – a demanding feat of physical endurance and one of Australia's premier wilderness walks.

Jeeps ferry hikers back and forth along this ice-age swathe, dotted with caves, quarries, basalt plains and Pleistocene archaeological sites.

Some of the world's largest carnivorous marsupials inhabit these regions, including the spotted-tailed quoll and the eastern quoll – two of the world's only three surviving monotremes. I, however, have my eyes peeled for a shy Tasmanian Devil, a creature rarely seen by humans in the wild. Since a rare cancer decimated numbers, this unique beast has almost been wiped from the radar. It remains unclear whether the Devil will survive the epidemic or, like the Tasmanian tiger, disappear into the world of legend and myth. I scour the forest for a stocky, black-and-white-flecked dog-like creature with a large boxy head, and hope.

Leaving the banks of the Meander River behind, I relish the ease of a day's cycling through level plains of crimson poppy fields. My bike and I are whizzing along at a fair old lick in perfect synchronicity and I can't help but feel a sense of smug achievement at the progress I am making – what a doddle! Not only was I well ahead of today's schedule, I haven't even broken a sweat and while the pinprick towns of Exton, Hagley, Carrick and Hadspen beckon, I've earmarked Westbury for a break. This elegant English-style town boasts some beautiful old buildings and I find sustenance in a homely tearoom packed with floral china and chintz. In what seems like ten minutes, I realise I've idled away an hour and gather up my belongings for fear of taking root. My lethargy is due, no doubt, to the hundredweight of jam-and-cream scones I've devoured. My euphoric get-up-and-go appears well and truly to have got-up-and-gone – a concern with over 32 kilometres (twenty miles) left to go. After adjusting my waistband, and with handlebars gripped, I lower my head, grit my teeth and feebly tap the pedals. Suffering the humiliation of being passed at speed by a wax-legged and well-oiled compatriot in super-swish Michael Roberts' garb, I can only gasp in awe at his disappearing profile and he whooshes by in a cloud of dust. Rising up out of the saddle, I push on determinedly Launceston-bound, realising that it's tricky to perfect that nonchalant 'whatever' look when you're struggling with a mouthful of flies.

After improving on a snail's pace, I finally screech to a triumphant halt in Launceston, propelled by gastronomic motivation. My rumbling stomach and I have picturesque Cataract Gorge as our goal, where I dine on mussels in bloom-filled gardens patrolled by strutting peacocks. Resplendent views and the gentle sound of the South Esk River are just the restorative therapy my body needs as I relax into a second glass of wine. The curious Tasmanian Devil may have eluded me, but I feel privileged to have encountered the magic of the island. Raising a glass to the joys of the earth's last great temperate wilderness, I feel a proud sense of achievement – and have the blisters as a badge of honour to prove it.

Endurance level: Moderate–Difficult

Tip: Slap on plenty of sunscreen – even on the cloudiest of days.

Contacts:
Island Cycle Tours
www.cycling-tasmania.com

Cycling Tasmania
www.tas.cycling.org.au

Bicycle Network Tasmania
www.biketas.org.au

THE AMERICAS

BIG ISLAND, HAWAII

With its remote location and paradisiacal beauty, Hawaii is the stuff of legends: an extraordinary collection of islands blessed with diverse landscapes and tropical splendour in a kaleidoscope of colours. For cyclists, the 'Big Island' offers the greatest two-wheeled pleasures on routes that pass time-carved lava fields, rainforests of vivid green, steep-sloped coffee plantations and truly gorgeous beaches. Serious cyclists will discover plenty of strenuous biking challenges, though there are some magical short leisure rides of less than twenty miles (32 kilometres) packed full of Hawaii adventure too. Abundant fresh Pacific Rim cuisine is perfect for powering cycling muscles, from the most succulent fish and seafood to nuts, honey and juicy tropical fruit. Take a trip out to Punaluu's black-sand beach and dramatic volcanic craters or try the 30-mile (48-kilometre) cycling course of the World Ironman Championships held on the unique molten rock terrain of Big Island.

Circumnavigating Big Island is to embark on a 300-mile (482-kilometre) loop around the coastal perimeter on a challenging climb up volcanic slopes with spellbinding views. At roughly the size of Los Angeles County, with two soaring peaks jutting up almost 14,000 feet (4,267 metres) towards the heavens, Big Island has arid desert scattered with dry scrub on its leeward side, while the windward is clad in dewy, hot, wet rainforest. Eleven different climatic zones lend

Photo: Lukas

the island a multitude of personalities: Celtic, Amazonian, Balinese, Saharan and Icelandic, to name just a few. Every bit of its scenery is theatrical and drama rich, from the weird black-lava extrusions that shoot towards the sky and the breathtaking descents that speed towards a coastline of the greenest blue. Dolphins, whales, sea turtles and a rainbow of fish swim among the coral. Sands range in colour from jet-black to silky white and yellow-green on beaches hemmed by lush emerald-coloured foliage. Sounds dreamy, doesn't it? It is. But if you prefer a nightmarish element, you'll find plenty of painful vertical ascents, most of them utterly brutal, on the Big Island's paved backroads.

Renting a bike by the day or week, or flying in your own, are both popular options. You're most likely to see cyclists of all types cruising around town on a basic model, pedalling along the shore on a tourer or doing battle with the volcano on a mountain bike. If you're hiring, you may prefer to bring your own pedals, shoes, helmets and seatbags. You'll also need to slather yourself with SPF50 sunblock (waterproof to reduce its sweating off); bring plenty with you because it is surprisingly hard to find away from the main tourist drag.

While circumnavigating the island, allow plenty of time for detours: delving down a lane or taking a lesser known backroad can often open up a whole new face of Hawaii. Rushing from destination to destination will mean missing out on some fascinating local encounters, such as sampling bizarre fruits on a roadside stall or joining local fishermen for breakfast at a small beachside cafe. Almost all the roads on the Big Island are scenic in their own way, but some are more special than others. My favourite is a seventeen-mile (27-kilometre) stretch west from the Volcano Village (towards Kona) that climbs the slopes above the Kīlauea Volcano. It takes you across old lava flows and through

Koa forests and boasts wide, expansive views across Hawaii Volcanoes National Park – it's hard not to cycle gape-mouthed in awestruck wonder.

Turn off the highway towards the mountain at the signposted exit to Mauna Loa (between mile markers 30 and 31) and follow it to the end – the road peters out to a mile-long scenic hiking trail. Leave your bike behind and don't forget to stop halfway up to look back to the mighty Kīlauea Volcano: the invigorating view is deserving of a photograph with its rounded boulders seemingly about to tumble down the brooding purple-black slopes.

On the doorstep of the Hawaii Volcanoes National Park lies one of the best kept secrets of the Big Island: Volcano Village: a rainforest village set amid towering ferns that is famous for its relaxing tranquillity. With access to many stunning hikes, the village is a perfect place to set up camp for a couple of days and explore some of the 500 square miles (805 square kilometres) of park designated as an International Biosphere Reserve (in 1980) and a UNESCO World Heritage Site (in 1987). From here, you will be able to witness flows of molten lava, sulphur banks, hot steam vents, ancient lava tubes and a huge summit caldera – and at an elevation of 4,000 feet the village is cool and breezy, a refreshing change from the climate along the Hawaiian coasts. Here the slow-paced rhythm of daily life is punctuated by thrilling sideswiping gusts and sharp, short climbs.

Stretches feel like you've pedalled back in time 30 years, onto an old country coastal byway – along lots of ups and downs, passing simple, old Hawaii houses, quiet fields and old stone bridges backdropped by woods and valleys. Needle-thin waterfall cascades bounce off green-black cliffs on a landscape of bleak, black lava on beautiful back roads that are free from traffic. Macadamia-nut groves and coffee plantations form dark forests and bushy farmland. Patches of light green grasslands dotted with cattle roll right down to a distant ocean.

Ferocious Hawaiian breezes send cotton-wool clouds scudding across wide open skies as you charge the hills for the promise of a glorious, downhill ride. In Big Island, to freewheel on a steep descent with the surf in view means an opportunity to hum the Hawaii 5-0 theme-tune with salt-spray on your cheeks and the wind in your hair.

Endurance level: Moderate–Difficult

Tip: Savour the downhill stretches of this thrilling ride; it's a real cobweb-buster!

Contacts:
Velissimo – Cycling Destinations Hawaii
www.cyclingdestinations.com/hawaii/cycling-hawaii

Hawaii Cycling Club
www.hawaiicyclingclub.com

Hawaii Tourism Board
www.gohawaii.com

UNDERGROUND RAILROAD ROUTE, USA–CANADA

It is dubbed the 'Mount Everest of cycling adventures' and, depending on who you speak to, is either 'a slice of paradise' or 'a piece of hell' – but one thing is certain, the historic

Underground Railroad Route is one of the longest cycling routes in the world. Comprising five different sections that add up to over 3,299 kilometres (2,050 miles), this USA-to-Canada stretch traces the route to freedom for slaves in the days before the Civil War. Easily dissectible legs allow cyclists to dip in for a day or spend a month or more enjoying this awesome trail, which runs from Mobile, Alabama in the southern USA to Owen Sound, Ontario in the north, with numerous cultural attractions along the way.

Often referred to as the Great Divide Bike Trail, this exhilarating route and its punishing terrain feature over 60,960 metres (200,000 feet) of elevation gain through some of the most remote and mountainous regions in North America. An ever-changing landscape, which runs parallel to the Continental Divide for a while, is not for the faint of heart: it crosses through some of the most diverse wilderness terrain a cyclist could encounter, much of it without services and amenities. Only the forest sites offer a degree of comfort with pit toilets and a water supply, while road surfaces vary from stretches of pavement and gravel roads to single-track mountain trails and crumbling old railroad beds to rocks and loose-stone trails. Not only is it tough on bikes, it is tough on joints, muscles and tendons. To complete the entire route takes about three months, during which time you'll likely encounter ice, snow, bears, wolves and rockfalls.

Grab guidebooks and detailed maps and speak to others who have ridden the Underground Railroad Route to help with planning this epic ride on a trail memorialising a network of clandestine routes used by African freedom-seekers to escape slavery before emancipation. Ragged thickets of sumac and maple trees hem the edge of a one-lane road, just as they may have lined the way to freedom two centuries ago. Shielded by the foliage, runaway slaves could

Photo: Artur Staszewski

silently slip into the shadows and make their escape across distant tobacco fields.

The route, a brainchild of the Adventure Cycling Association (ACA), helps modern-day visitors understand this cardinal chapter of America's past, mapping the trail for thousands of miles with stops along the way to illustrate the story of the fleeing slaves. Once trains stopped running in the 1970s, the route became overgrown until the intervention of the ACA. Today, more than 4,500 maps of the route have been sold since it was released in 2007, indicating that cyclists relish this glute-busting way to experience the tragic and heroic stories of history. Fugitives, of course, would do the whole thing on foot while being pursued by armed men with dogs and there are poignant reminders of this as you pedal along between the Deep South and Canada. Following rivers through Alabama, Mississippi, Tennessee and Kentucky before crossing into Ohio, the route then leaves the river to head toward Lake Erie and enters Canada at the Peace Bridge in Buffalo, New York. In Ontario, it then follows the shores of Lake Ontario and ends at Owen Sound, a town on the southern side of Lake Huron's Georgian Bay founded by freedom seekers as early as 1843.

The southernmost map begins in historic Mobile, Alabama – once a key port for slave ships from Africa. Road plaques detail sites of massacres, German prisoner-of-war camps and the last major battle of the Civil War at Blakeley State Park. Pedal past town squares with courthouses and Confederate memorials, tall loblolly pines and the brown waters of the slow-moving Tombigbee and Tennessee rivers. Steep, short roller-coaster hills welcome you to the area of western Tennessee and Kentucky rich in Civil War battlefields and history. Bison-filled woodlands and bird-rich riverbanks hail the route turning north-east along the Ohio River, once known as the dividing line between the slave and free states. Here, helpers would slip back into slave territory to help freedom seekers find their way, while others provided much-needed shelter to runaways. From here towards Miami, the trail winds through rolling farmlands, picturesque towns, river cliffs and hardwood forests – though you're unlikely to have many human companions, you'll have warblers and other songbirds all around you, together with snatched glimpses of whitetail deer, coyote and beaver.

This is in sharp contrast to Ohio's capital, Columbus, where higher levels of traffic pound the route to the north-east to Oberlin, Hudson and Ashtabula. As the home of one of the first colleges in the USA to admit African-American students, Oberlin is also where you'll find the First Church of Oberlin, which served as the headquarters of the Oberlin Anti-Slavery Society. Hudson is where the early abolitionist movement gained momentum and was the first town in northern Ohio to receive a state Underground Railroad historical marker, while Ashtabula was once a place of hidden safe houses. The Buffalo/Niagara area became a natural funnel for freedom seekers, due to its remoteness, its proximity to Canada and the anti-slavery sentiment that ran strong throughout New York state. One of Buffalo's best-known Underground Railroad sites is the Michigan Avenue Baptist Church. In the 1850s, the church building served as an Underground Railroad safe house, where freedom seekers would hide in the basement waiting to be boated across the Niagara River to Canada in the safety of darkness.

After crossing into Canada, from Fort Erie to Niagara-on-the-Lake, the route mainly uses a trail along the Niagara River. This part of the route necessitates good planning as everything near Niagara Falls is extremely busy in summer and accommodation becomes as scarce as gold-dust in a USA gold rush fever. Owen Sound, known as the final terminal of the Underground Railroad, is where many former slaves found their hard-earned freedom. Today the village formerly known as Sydenham has a fascinating slave ancestry and hosts an Emancipation Picnic each year; in 2017 it will celebrate its 155th year. The party also honours two great historic milestones of freedom: the British Emancipation Act of 1834 and the United States Emancipation Proclamation of 1863. Expect community song, prayer and much food, dancing and family fun.

Endurance level: Moderate

Tip: History lovers will adore the heritage to be found on this odyssey through time.

Contacts:
Greater Niagara Tourism
www.greaterniagara.com

Underground Railroad Museum
www.undergroundrailroadmuseum.org

Ontario Tourism
www.ontariotravel.net

SAN JUAN ARCHIPELAGO, USA

Though North American cyclists are no strangers to the scenic joys of the San Juan Archipelago, to the rest of the world it remains largely unknown. A short jaunt from America's west coast ensures a steady succession of two-wheeled arrivals from Seattle and Vancouver (British Columbia) who take to the quiet rural roads of the islands to enjoy long sunny days, low rainfall (only half that of Seattle), magnificent views and an incredible abundance of wildlife. More than 170 atolls and islets lie in the rain shadow of the Olympic Mountains, offering a wide variety of cycling experiences, from self-guided solo trips to fully supported group tours. Numerous hire firms rent out premium bicycles and an array of cycling gear, so those who decide to travel light and arrive on foot are well catered for. Trips that are fully supported are accompanied by an equipment van, guides and GPS/tele-communications. Bike route maps can be picked up free at every turn. Few destinations can claim to be as cycling-friendly. In fact, there is only one thing more popular than cycling on the San Juan Archipelago: the thrills and joys of the sea.

Rich in a history of early Coast Salish settlements and Captain Vancouver's explorations, the past, present and future of the San Juan Islands has an inextricable maritime link. Sailboats, yachts, kayaks and old-fashioned schooners cruise the very same waters that mariners, pirates and pioneers sailed in bygone times. During the whale-watch season, the entire archipelago becomes a place of homage for the islands' magnificent monsters of the deep. Lime Kiln Point on the rocky western side of San Juan Island is one of the best land-based orca-watching viewpoints – it's reachable via a rugged route by bike for truly awesome sightseeing in-the-saddle.

Of all the islands in the archipelago, San Juan, Orcas and Lopez are the favourite to explore by bike: San Juan offers a little level of difficulty, Orcas Island has more challenging

rides and Lopez Island has the flattest terrain. Though the temperature on the islands is mild year-round, it still gets cold in the winter months, so the prime time to arrive on bicycle is from spring to autumn. The Lonely Planet ranked the San Juan Islands as its top US destination when it compiled a Top 10 list of cycling routes. The three-island chain also plays host to many charity bike rides each year, with each island served by the dirt-cheap Washington State Ferry System – leave your car in Anacortes and board with just your bicycle to enjoy the freedom of nicely paved rural roads and designated bicyclist rest and picnic areas. Stick inland for the gentlest rides or head to the scenic shoreline for the hilliest bike routes. For the ultimate ascent, cyclists can test their legs on Mount Constitution: the steepest climb on the archipelago's highest point (elevation 2,409 feet) on Orcas Island.

Don't be fooled by the slow-paced gentle roads because these often lead to gruelling hills that leave calves tingling. Lopez Island, with its stunning water views at the north and south ends, can be comfortably cycled in a day, with plenty of stop-offs at parks and beaches for picnics, wildlife viewing or short hikes. For a compact isle, at just 24 kilometres (fifteen miles) long, Lopez offers a richly woven tapestry of contrasting landscapes, from bird-scattered forests, wave-lapped bays and beaches strewn with driftwood to distant views of Mount Baker's snow-tipped peak. Lopez's natural beauty and quality of life attracted Scandinavian farmers here in the 1850s. Today, the meadows, pasture and farmland support an eclectic agricultural community, from cheese-makers, llama farmers and fishermen to those engaged in apple orchards, wineries, and making jams and preserves.

San Juan Island is a more challenging island circum-navigation: the loop and two scenic legs are less than 81 kilometres (50 miles), but riding the terrain is a thigh-burning workout, with beautiful beaches a reward for the slog.

Only experienced cyclists should attempt the squiggly, narrow roads of Orca Island: a curving, snaking 92-kilometre (57-mile) route through a rural idyll past fruit fields, farmsteads, woodlands and old wooden barns. Tight lanes demand an extraordinary sustained level of concentration and with frequent oh-so-steep gradients and very few rest stops are physically tough too. Serious cycling nuts make a beeline for Mount Constitution to embark on the slow climb up to its peak. As the archipelago's highest mountain, views from the summit are jaw-dropping across a patchwork of a zillion different greens on America's self-proclaimed 'Emerald Isle'.

Drivers on the archipelago are familiar with the roads and safe passing opportunities and are respectful of cyclists. Visiting cyclists should obey traffic laws and anticipate pinch points, ride defensively and wear appropriate high-visibility clothing. Purpose-built pull-over spots enable cyclists to pull off the road safely. Given the nature of the roads, wearing a helmet is advisable. Some roads carry warnings for cyclists because they do not carry the width, fog lines or paved shoulders on long grades and sharp curves with shortened sight lines. These roads, especially in inclement weather or summer months with increased traffic, require special caution and defensive cycling, but signs by the road highlight this. On the most bucolic stretches, another potential hazard is the archipelago's wildlife: inland there are deer, eagles and black foxes, while along the coast seals, otters, sea lions and, of course, whales are likely distractions to cyclists with one eye on the road.

Endurance level: Easy

Tip: Avoid this trip in the harsh winter and instead enjoy the beautiful cycling conditions in spring, summer and autumn.

Contacts:
San Juan Tourism
www.visitsanjuans.com

Island Bicycles
www.islandbicycles.com

TRANSAMERICA TRAIL, USA

Nature-freaks who are up for a challenge should consider following the TransAmerica Trail, which cuts straight through the Yellowstone and Grand Teton National Parks. As a favourite route that has been ridden by hard-core cyclists for years, the TransAmerica Trail has spawned all manner of cafes, restaurants and overnight accommodation along the way – regular cross-country riders with a good history of the route always spot lots of different stuff year-on-year. Most allow around three months (give or take) to do the Trail, start to finish – do it any quicker and you risk it passing in a scenic blur.

The official start of the TransAmerica Trail is Astoria, Oregon, the oldest permanent settlement on America's Pacific Coast located at the mouth of the Columbia River, where glorious stretches of sandy beaches trimmed by seafood restaurants are great preparation for the upcoming steep ascents and descents. The route begins to truly test your stamina once it has turned inland to the Willamette River Valley. Eugene is the largest city along the route, with

Missoula (Montana), Pueblo (Colorado) and Carbondale (Illinois) other sizeable cities along the way. Diverse eco-climates form a checkerboard along the trail with the lush, green western side of the Cascade Mountains a startling contrast to the dry terrain after McKenzie Pass. Spikes, twists and ragged caves characterise the crossing at McKenzie Pass, which slices through an ancient lava field with its weird, wonderful Gothic shades of grey and black and dried molten rivers. Spectacular views abound across the Three Sisters in all their sibling glory – Big Sister (Faith), Middle Sister (Charity) and Little Sister (Hope) characterise the dry, crumbling peaks once travelled by America's early pioneers.

Idaho offers a wonderful ride along the Salmon River, and some interesting Native American historic sites to visit. The route then follows the winding, scenic Lochsa River for the longest gradual ascent of the trip (around 70 miles/113 kilometres). You'll climb up and over Lolo Pass in the Bitterroot Range of the northern Rocky Mountains to enter the neighbouring state of Montana, from which you'll reach the spur into Missoula approximately 40 miles (64 kilometres) west-south-west. This laid-back college town provides one of the highlights of the route for cyclists: it has an Adventure Cycling headquarters with its 'cyclist's lounge' and other amenities for road-weary pedal-pounders of the road. After some much-needed R&R absorbing blissful panoramas of wide, sweeping valleys scattered with butterflies and birds, you will feel fully rejuvenated. Nature is a magical healer in this beauty-rich, tranquil place – it is hard to believe you're only sixteen hours away from the celebrity fakery, red-carpet glitz, limousines, gridlocked traffic and cosmetic surgeons of Hollywood.

Most cyclists embarking on this epic 90-day two-wheeled slog have set aside plenty of time to drink in the views at Yellowstone National Park and the Grand Teton Range in

Photo: Carol M. Highsmith

Wyoming, where incomparable landscapes deserve at least two or three days out of the saddle. You can store your bike if you'd prefer to stretch your legs on a hike around the National Park: information points have maps, guides and details of accommodation close by and can help with practical stuff like providing a luggage locker.

There are plenty of countryside routes to enjoy, dotted with picket-fenced farmsteads, while the historic settlements of Dubois and Lander boast plenty of Western charm with their country ballads and western-style cooking. Lamont is an oasis in the windy, desolate Great Divide Basin – stop here for a cold beer, views across dusty cactus-strewn arid plains and a seriously good bowl of chili.

On the approach to Kremmling, Colorado, the scenery shifts a gear into alpine mode to leave the dry, high desert way behind. Alpine splendour abounds here and the drop in temperature helps as you begin the cool, long climb up through the snow-covered slopes to the crest of the Continental Divide at Hoosier Pass at 11,542 feet (3,518 metres). At the point that the route prepares to leave the Rockies, Royal Gorge Park offers the options of a helicopter ride or raft trip across the white-tipped waters of the magnificent, cavernous gorge – an awesome spectacle. Pueblo offers cyclists the luxury of a good bike repair shop close to some great little places to eat. It also denotes the halfway point of the TransAm Trail and, with plenty of bars in which to raise a glass to reaching the milestone, this is a cool place to overnight. Congratulations – you have now clocked up more than 2,500 miles (4,023 kilometres).

The journey into the eastern part of Colorado as you cross into western Kansas turns distinctly hot and dry. Prepare to cycle across some fine barren country with plenty of water in your panniers, a decent sunhat and the highest factor sunblock you can find. It is here, close to Haswell, Colorado, that you wave farewell to the last hazy glimpse of the Rocky Mountains. These fabled peaks stretch some 3,000 miles (4,828 kilometres) from British Columbia and Alberta in Canada through Idaho, Montana, Wyoming, Colorado, running down to New Mexico in the USA. If ever there was a spot for a selfie, this is it – on a famous ridged backdrop of the most dramatic wilderness landscape sprinkled with silvery snow and traversed by numerous hiking trails.

To escape the midday heat of cycling in Kansas, most road-tripping bikers set off at first light and spend their afternoons taking cool dips in a pool. Early evening rides are pleasant too, with potentially several hours to make up the miles in cooler temperatures before the dark of nightfall.

The flat-as-a-pancake cycle paths that cut through the Great Plains undergo a major transformation on the approach to Missouri. From here the route becomes a lung-busting roller-coaster through eye-catching scenery that offers adventure sports (canoeing, rock climbing and abseiling) and Civil War history and plenty of deep, cool-water swimming holes until it crosses the Mississippi River at Chester, Illinois. From the college town of Carbondale, with its coffee bars, bookshops and night clubs, take a ferry across the Ohio River into Kentucky to enjoy some downtime with the fireflies around a campfire, sipping strong coffee on a backdrop of rolling white-fenced pasture and woodlands. The town of Berea marks the gateway to the soaring Appalachian Mountains and its rich folklore and legends. For some time out of the saddle, enjoy a troglodyte tour of the Mammoth Cave National Park, the world's longest subterranean cave system with its vast colonies of bats in a part of the Green River valley and hilly country of south-central Kentucky.

Past Berea, the trail rolls into a syncopated rhythm of

long, gruelling ascents followed by an exhilarating downhill freewheel that more than makes up for the pain of the climb. This is the way to truly ride the Appalachians! Part of the route incorporates a stretch of the Blue Ridge Parkway in Virginia: a National Parkway and All-American Road noted for its scenic beauty that runs 469 miles (755 kilometres) as America's longest linear park.

After a couple of hours, the mountains begin to level out into gentle rolling hills before the landscape becomes a flat land of pasture, meadows and lush plantations. Numerous signposts detail side-trips and excursions to explore the rich history of the American Revolution – Colonial Williamsburg is undoubtedly the highlight, with its English heritage as part of the well-preserved Historic Triangle, which attracts more than 4 million history buffs a year.

After three months on the road, crossing through hundreds of towns and pedalling for well over 4,200 miles (6,759 kilometres), the settlement of Yorktown is in sight. Situated on the attractive estuary town of Chesapeake Bay, this historic town marks the end of your mammoth trans-national two-wheeled trek across America's girth. On the approach to Chesapeake Bay, it is customary for road-warrior cyclists to ride triumphantly into town with arms aloft before enjoying a celebratory slap-up meal of seafood at the legendary beer haunt Skippers Pier. Cheers!

Endurance level: Difficult

Tip: Two-wheeling this route is a great way to meet cycling comrades from all over the world.

Contacts:
Trans-America Trail

www.transamtrail.com

Trans Am Bike Race
www.transambikerace.com

KINGDOM TRAILS, USA

For a state that's only 200 miles (321 kilometres) long and
a fraction of that distance wide, Vermont has an estimated
1,000 miles(1,609 kilometres) of single-track mountain bike
trails, ranging from tree-root-riddled earthy tracks to dirt
trails strewn with rocks and debris. Village-to-village country
roads are perfect for two wheels, while an extensive network
of lightly trafficked small-town roads are favourite routes
for tours. Off-road gravel and old logging trails characterise
some of the best mountain biking in the USA. Race through
snaking forest paths, across fluffy pasture or down swooping
hills full of switchbacks: this is adventure-packed mountain
biking at its most awesome (just unfurling the map makes
you want to high-five!).

Rushing across slippery bark and fluttery leaf litter
through woodland ferns is pure elation at the Kingdom
Trails, where plenty of rollable fallen trees offer the chance
of airtime, if you fancy it. Sandy soil and foliage ensure soft
landings on meticulously maintained trails that run for
miles and miles. A hundred miles to be precise. Choose
from numerous looping beginner and intermediate trails
on an expansive acreage of woodlands that can easily keep
any level rider busy for an hour or two. Few riders manage
to follow the exact same route twice, in the tentacle-like

Photo: Patrick McCaffrey

Kingdom Trails. A giant, counter-clockwise loop is suitable for an intermediate speed freak who likes to catch air in numerous unorthodox ways. After a few miles of paved road to the top of the hill, beyond a beautiful farm, the trail network can be seen heading left. After a gentle stretch in the saddle, it is time for a riveting downhill trail called 'Tap & Die': a ridiculously fun, fast and furious downhill roller-coaster blast with sweeping curves. You'll hear the hoot and holler through the forest of anyone on the descent.

Turn left at the exit of 'Tap & Die' at the first bend to 'River Run', where there's a great cedar-trimmed swimming hole for a cooling dip. Next on to the spiralling flow through the sparse pine forest on 'Old Webbs', where aggressive riding across bumps and ridges leads to a major intersection. Head onto 'Hog Back', then left onto 'Sidewinder', which has been described as the single-track mountain bike equivalent of an Olympic-size snowboard half pipe (an epic semi-circular ditch on a downward slope), up to 22 feet (6.5 metres) deep. Survive this? Then be sure to climb up 'West Branch' and do it again – everyone in the know insists twice is a MUST.

From the top of 'West Branch' hit the two 'Border' side trails and then onto 'Jaw', 'Maxilla' and 'Sugar Hill' before nipping up to 'Ridge' then whizzing down to 'Rim' in a rapid cross-country rally. By the turn right up to 'East Branch', you'll be feeling the burn in your thighs as you turn right again onto 'Easy Out' and again onto 'Vast'. Grab some air before heading to 'Connector', then cruise comfortably down 'Pines'. Here you'll cross into 'Vast' again on a straight, fast run through a proud regiment of trees until you screech to halt at a T-junction. Take a right to one of the Kingdom Trails machine-built tracks, 'Kitchel' – an out-and-out blast among ferns and bracken. Pedal hard and fast as you speed through the jumps and race towards the pretty East Burke Village.

In the heart of the North-east Kingdom of Vermont, this exciting maze of trails was created in 1994 to help promote the natural beauty of the region. Primarily a volunteer-driven endeavour, Kingdom Trails is one of the most magnificent networks of mountain bike paths in North America. Mixing easy-going cross-country tours with heart-in-the-mouth free-ride descents, all 100 miles (161 kilometres) offer a chance to hit incredible lines on a host of hills and slopes – with each one linking into the other (and better than the last). Beginners will enjoy the range of soft forest terrain, while the pros will revel in the hard-rocking jumps and obstacle-blocked paths. Lunch spots, swimming holes and uplifting scenery are the perfect combination for first-rate fun – you'll leave Kingdom Trails muddy, but smiling, sure that you'll want to come back.

Looking to stay nearby? The Burke area is a four-season destination with every outdoor pursuit covered and a host of accommodation options to suit every budget, from country inns, B&Bs, resorts and self-catering rental homes. Hiking, boating, fishing, paddling, swimming, rock climbing and horse-riding are also popular in Burke, where the Great Outdoors is king. Mountain biking has won it a cabinet full of accolades and awards: *USA Today* has named the Kingdom Trails one of the 'Top Ten Places to Mountain Bike'.

An unpretentious local mountain bike scene has pioneered the sport of winter biking – the newest snow-slope craze. Great news for anyone who may feel downbeat when the cycling season ends as soon as the big freeze beings. Winter biking is a slip-sliding success at the Kingdom Trails. Trails offer even greater peace and solitude after a heavy snowfall and boast an ethereal beauty when draped in cloaks of powdery white. Specially selected fat bike trails race across the single-track mountain biking trails on the East Side of

Darling Hill, together with a host of favourite summertime trails available all winter long. Atmospheric and alluring, the snowy trails weave among nature's frosted chandeliers and crystal icicle cascades as the heart starts pumping, the blood starts flowing, the calories start burning. Few things are as exhilarating, or memorable, as bundling yourself up in the warmest gear to ride through deep drifts of snow, glistening ice or freezing bullets of rain.

Endurance level: Moderate

Tip: Have your camera at the ready as you pound the pedals – the views are amazing.

Contacts:
Kingdom Trails
www.kingdomtrails.org

Visit Vermont
www.visit-vermont.com

MIAMI, USA

Miami's sassy cycling scene is blessed with a seductive mix of trails, from the ocean-front paths packed with bikes and inline skaters to the funky little cycle routes that capture Art Deco, history and celebrity culture. Miami's affinity for two-wheeled travel may not compare with Amsterdam or many other European cities, but with year-round biking weather, an overdose of natural beauty and a flat terrain, the city's cycle culture is evolving rapidly. Trails suit recreational bicyclists, not athletic stamina, but eliminate the worries and dangers of Miami traffic. And with pretty scenery to enjoy, and places to see and stop along the way, a growing number of tourists are pumping up their tyres, grabbing a helmet and discovering hidden roads for true neighbourhood exploration.

More and more curious cyclists are delving into Old Cutler Trail, which runs from Coral Gables along a flawless paved path and stretches for eleven miles (eighteen kilometres) for a calm and beautiful ride under the banyan trees. Pick up Old Cutler Trail at its northern trailhead at the traffic circle where Old Cutler Road, Sunset Road and Le Jeune Road converge. The southern trailhead is located at the junction of SW 87th Avenue and Old Cutler Road in Cutler Bay. From its southern end, you can connect to the 2.7-mile (4.3-kilometre) Biscayne Trail, which provides a pleasant route down to Biscayne Bay.

The trail winds past secluded estates with high, vine-covered stucco walls that were once owned by drug lords, exiled dictators and pop royalty – Madonna famously lived here next door to Sylvester Stallone's grand mansion. Gardens bursting with crimson bougainvillea, yellow bromeliads and huge, hand-shaped palms draw you along this splendid back-route, built between 1916 and 1919. Considerate conservation of architecture and landmarks has ensured that Coral Gables' unique past as one of America's first fully-planned communities is still evident today. Incorporating secluded residential enclaves and commercial areas inspired by the architectural style of the Mediterranean, the concept behind Coral Gables was to mix the natural environment with buildings with an international flavour. In addition, Coral Gables has been named a 'Tree City USA' for 26 consecutive

Photo: Marc Averette

years due its beautiful green spaces and comprehensive parks and recreation programmes. Certainly, Old Cutler Road offers plenty of visual pleasures, as well as numerous stops where you can stretch your legs, and presents an alternative character to the fast-paced image of Miami as a 'Manhattan with palm trees'.

Yet Old Cutler Road is a mere few blocks behind strip malls, billboards and traffic lanes of the harrowing US 1. It is hard to imagine that, just five minutes' drive from Le Jeune Road, you can reach something that resembles Jurassic Park. The Old Cutler Zone offers an opportunity to journey through some of the most beautiful neighbourhoods in the greater Miami area, along a tree-studded trail that passes foliage-packed parks and gardens of soaring palms for its entire length.

Spend time at the Matheson Hammock Park, Miami's oldest park, for restful views out across Biscayne Bay and Miami's dramatic skyline. A beautiful grassy meadow has a scenic pond with belly flopping iguanas, a small mangrove forest and a few hardwood trees, a resplendent coconut-palmed lagoon and exquisite seafood at the Red Fish Grill, a historic building made of coral. Or stroll through the fragrant flower beds of the resplendent Fairchild Tropical Garden, established in 1936 by plant enthusiasts David Fairchild and Robert H. Montgomery, and opened to the public in 1938. Rated by *Miami Herald* as the 'top Florida wonder', it is the largest tropical botanical garden in the USA (at 83 acres/35.5 hectares) and one of Miami's most scenic attractions – and home to the only outdoor tropical rainforest in the continental USA, a floral paradise full of exotic plants and a rainbow of blousey blooms. Next it is Pinecrest Gardens, full of more vivid horticultural delights with its enthusiastic squirrels, squawking birds and whimsical well-manicured modern gardens: a wonderful mix of old and new, of spectacles both man-made and natural, that echoes the widespread appeal of Old Cutler Trail.

You will also find that the trail plays host to cycling events such as fundraising bike rides and block parties led by Miami's A-list names, such as six miles (9.5 kilometres) with NBA superstar Dwyane Wade at the front of the pack. Organised by the Miami Bike Scene as a massive bike 'parade' to draw attention to the bikeability of many of the neighbourhoods of the city, events such as these attract many thousands of participants to Coral Gable's canopied trails. It also runs free weekly group rides and has a full directory all of the bike rental shops, cycle repair stores, bike tour specialists and cycle-friendly cafes, hotels and restaurants plus a comprehensive calendar of events of everything from bike sales to cycling buddy groups and social events.

Endurance level: Easy

Tip: Enjoy the opportunity to pick up speed on this trip – surfaces are flat, slick, well maintained and a joy to ride.

Contacts:
Miami Bike Scene
www.themiamibikescene.com

Miami Tourist Board
www.miamiandbeaches.com

Coral Cables
www.coralgables.com

LA FAROLA, CUBA

An island nation spanning over 42,000 square miles (67,593 square kilometres), Cuba boasts more than 3,500 miles (5,633 kilometres) of Caribbean coastline with the Straits of Florida to the north. At over 780 miles (1,255 kilometres) long and 119 miles (191 kilometres) wide across its widest points, it is certainly no small landmass. 'Phew, it's a lot bigger than I thought', I gulped, as I studied a map before deciding – wisely – to scale down my cycling ambitions. I'm drawn to Cuba's eastern and southern flank as this stretch has become an increasingly popular tour route with cyclists in-the-know. With dramatic scenery and traffic-free roads, this segment of Cuba includes the epic and exhilarating ride over La Farola and a magnificent ride along the southern coast.

As Cuba's highest mountain road, La Farola is an engineering feat of the brave new Cuba of the early 1960s. It is a route that curls through Guantánamo province: an unlikely tourist destination. Cutting through sun-crisped arid scrub and dusty cacti of the desolate coastal strip around US-controlled land and 'that' bay, the steep climb up towards La Farola has been described as a 'landscape on steroids' due to its awe-packed wow. The scenery is incredible: a long stretch of rolling beaches, mountain landscapes and cathedral spires marking out the distant city skylines. La Farola means 'the lighthouse' in Spanish, which is a clue to how high and exposed it is.

As the first stage of the Vuelta Ciclista a Cuba (Cuba's version of the Tour de France), this is no easy-peasy pedal. It runs for almost six miles (over nine kilometres) from the tip of the Baracoa Mountains on a succession of skinny spiral switchbacks with perilous limestone ledges. Cuba's eastern region was the heartland of the Cuban Revolution and is a place renowned for its firebrand politics and national pride. As you ride along the edge of death-defying drops, the Caribbean looms large and brilliant-blue as a nerve-calming distraction. With no guardrails as such, just some flimsy-looking metal fencing, it feels as if the bike is moments from skidding off the edge of the world as the descent gains pace. Thankfully, freewheeling fear subsides with the many small uphill slogs that punctuate the route and avid cyclists soon appreciate why La Farola is rated by cyclists worldwide as one of the most rewarding routes in Cuba. Since construction of the road was completed in the 1960s, accessing the country's mountainous eastern terrain has become a challenge to cyclists with enough stamina to propel themselves along its tight cliff-side turns. It's hot, your quads burns, your heart pounds, your lungs burst and you may well emit a high-pitched shriek on the high-velocity downhill stretches. Throughout it all, I drew some comfort from the thrilling views offered by the serrated slopes of the mountains, however strenuous the pedalling.

The blazing sun is unrelenting, but I'm cheered by the sight of a few woolly clouds above a string of deep-green forested hills. As I approach a cloud-topped wooded glade, the rain pelts the road like a hail of bullets, torrential and cool after the morning's heat. It stops in an instant, but is wonderfully refreshing none the less. I watch bright blue and yellow butterflies dance around the foliage and marvel once again at the colours of the terrain. The stillness is beautiful, peaceful.

Every now and again, a lone vehicle wheezes past me in an unsuitable gear. With a rattle of complaint, and a smoky belch of refusal, a small flat-bed truck grinds dramatically to

Photo: Christian Pirkl

a halt on a dogleg turn. Pressing my face to the handlebars, I whisper a prayer to the gods. I'm thankful that, at 1805 feet (550 metres) above sea level up a mountain, my bike isn't rebelling too. For while some of the route has been paved, much of the descent has been littered with potholes (baches). I watch ox and horses navigate vast holes the size of a double bed with nimble-hoofed precision. Unfortunately, where there is livestock, there is also manure – and lots of it. I almost preferred the potholes to the great steaming piles of poop.

Cuba is tropical, with a hurricane season that lasts from June to November, so you will probably want to stick to March to May (warm and dry) or December to February (warm and humid). January is the coolest month, but in reality the seasonal temperature variation is minimal.

Cubans are extremely friendly people and with quiet roads and cheap accommodation it is easy to tour there on a budget. Food can be hard to find, so ask your B&B or hotel to pack up a lunchtime picnic and snacks. Without these, you're reliant on food stores that sell to foreign visitors – and not all do. It has taken a while for the Cuban tourism industry to realise that not all international visitors want to spend a week holed away in an all-inclusive resort, away from everyday Cubans. It is still difficult for non-locals to buy fresh food, although there are some fruit vendors and street stalls in town centres. Keep a stash of nuts, biscuits and crackers in your pack, just in case you're caught out.

If you speak some Spanish, however basic, it's very useful because very few Cubans speak English. However, they are expressive and communicative people, so body language and common understanding does go far. Be aware that Cuba does not have standard ATMs, so you will need cash to exchange. Obtain two currencies: Convertible pesos (1

Convertible peso = approx. US$1) designated for use by tourists and Cuban pesos (25 Cuban pesos = approx. US$1). I spent about US$30 a day. Money stretches a long way because Cubans can fix, adapt, mend and recycle anything – a huge comfort to cyclists. Getting bike frames welded, tyres repaired, inner tubes mended and ripped panniers stitched has never been easier than in Cuba, a country that is full of ingenious menders well-practised at making do.

Endurance level: Moderate

Tip: Pack a decent puncture kit (or three) – the road surface is heavily pitted in parts.

Contacts:
Cuba Cycle Tours
www.cubacycletours.com

Intrepid Travel
www.intrepidtravel.com

BLUE MOUNTAIN/FERN GULLY, JAMAICA

Keen to soak up the relaxed vibe of Jamaica well away from the bustle? Then it pays to seek out the quietude of the countryside and stick to the lesser known backroads. Give the tourist areas a wide berth for peace and quality, especially Montego Bay, because that's where the hustlers go. Instead, explore the peaceful rural lanes that lead to tranquil, crowd-free beaches. With its British colonial past,

Jamaica also boasts a long cycling history, so there is no need to rely on gas guzzling SUVs for transport. Plenty of bike rental and tour operators operate across the island, together with several cycling guides that offer trips out across a scenic mix of gentle terrain, forested mountains, coastal routes and rolling green hills.

In recent years, Jamaica's cycling scene has benefited from the momentum inspired by island cyclists Dr Franklyn Bennett, Paul Andrew Goldson and Tim Byam. As the brains behind Jamaica's leading amateur cycling event, the trio have grabbed the attention of the cycling public and today the Jamaica By Bike ride is an annual fixture on the cycling calendar. As the dynamo behind greater cycling collaboration, the event sparked Caribbean-wide interest in Jamaica's cycling routes and future potential. Today, the Jamaica Cycling Federation promotes cycling throughout the island, focusing on mountain bike, road and track – some of the island's most enthusiastic biking tour guides have worked for, or with, this lottery-funded foundation.

Cyclists in Jamaica are regarded with fond affection. Children wave and grown men gather round to check out the latest spec, customised frames or snazzy extras. There are always plenty of jokes and quips flying around about cycling, as you'd expect from a nation that prides itself on its humour. For example: 'Hey mon, d'ya know why a bicycle can't stand up on its own? Because it too tyred!' Bicycles, just like cars in Jamaica, are subject to the rules of the road, though nobody takes much notice of stop signs and traffic signals, so you'll need to keep your wits about you. Potholes, hazards (branches in the road) and road obstructions (anything from roaming goats or broken down minivans) are common wherever you are in Jamaica. A helmet and a puncture repair kit are essential, even on the shortest trip.

For the most adventurous mountain bike speed freaks, be sure to contact the crew behind the Jamaica Fat Tyre Festival – the island's wildest mass participation cycling event. These guys run bespoke tours too and are a great fun way to experience Jamaica: you don't need to have pro skills to enjoy the fast-paced downhill velocity in a palm-fringed exotic location, just reasonably fit. One of the most exciting full-day rides on the island centres on the 7,402-foot (2,256-metre) peaks of the Blue Mountain, the highest in the English-speaking Caribbean. Coping with the elevation on a climb that comes in at less than ten miles (seventeen kilometres) ensures cyclists are faced with one of the steepest and most punishing gradients on the planet. As your thighs burn and the vein in your forehead begins to bulge like an overstuffed sausage, you realise that it's not called mountain biking without good reason.

On the foothills, the terrain throws everything at you on the early ascent: soft and loamy tracks, rocky ledges, twisted tree roots the size of truck tyres, thick mud, dry stretches of sand, a carpet of decomposing mangoes and roaming livestock. Goats, cows, donkeys and umpteen flapping, squawking birds appear from nowhere. In every respect, Jamaican cycling trails are living, breathing things that alter with every season and change shape with each burst of rain. Lizards scuttle among small rocks where yellow snakes soak up the sun, while all around delicate, shimmering hummingbirds flit and flutter. Tree frogs chirp, small monkeys emit their terrifying shrieks and parrots rustle the leaves, so your nerves may suffer as much as your leg muscles. The descent is well earned for the sheer pain of hitting the uphill trails. The charm of the small villages, beautiful vistas and cool waterfall cascades make the experience sublime and the challenging hairpin bends and hair-raising free-

Photo: Wolmadrian

wheeling stretches ensure the Blue Mountains ride is utterly unforgettable.

Staying in capital city Kingston and keen to escape the suffocating heat? Then take a scenic ride out to leafy Bog Walk Gorge with family-run outfit Jamaica By Bike. The route traverses the historic Flat Bridge along the fern-topped banks of the boulder-strewn Rio Cobre to Bog Walk before a gradual climb over Mount Rosser. A fast-paced descent into Moneague leads through scenic Fern Gully with its gorgeous soaring tropical blooms and extraordinary birds. Thought to have once been an underground river flowing through caves, the roofs of which later collapsed, beautiful Fern Gully with its forested banks and orbs of sponge-like moss has an other-worldly feel. Chinks of golden sunlight form brilliant laser beams through the foliage that shoots and sprouts from every rocky crevice and fissure. Branches interlaced with vines grow bound with a tangle of creepers, parasitical plants and suckers are scattered with flowers in bright red, white, yellow and purple. This enchanting setting, with its giant nodding ferns, has a magical glow and stretches from Ocho Rios to the community of Colgate. Over 300 varieties of towering fern form a shady tunnel of lush greenery together with other woodland species and the banana palm: the perfect place for a rest from the saddle.

Endurance level: Easy–Moderate

Tip: Don't rely on signage or markers for turn-offs and junctions as typically only large roads are signed.

Contacts:
Jamaica By Bike
www.jamaicabybike.com

Jamaica Cycling Federation
www.jamaicacycling.com

Singletrack Jamaica
www.singletrackjamaica.com

TINKER TRAIL, ST LUCIA

Two-wheeling in the Caribbean is a rewarding way to sightsee
the islands, if you aren't a holidaymaker who likes to flop
and drop. Contrary to all the marketing blurb, a Caribbean
holiday can be an active one. Quiet roads and numerous
tour options, from self-guided bike hire to organised trips,
ensure cycling is easily arranged. Most destinations offer an
array of bikes to suit every ability and age, with itineraries that
range from short family tours to gruelling slogs up towering
mountain peaks high above the Caribbean Sea. Cool breezes
and unbeatable views of rainforests, plantations and palm-
fringed shores ensure plenty of diversions along the way.

On the beautiful island of St Lucia, exploring on a bicycle
is typically done along scenic roughshod mountain biking
trails. At just 27 miles (44 kilometres) long and fourteen
miles (25 kilometres) wide, St Lucia isn't overwhelming for
intermediate cyclists and beginners – and that is part of its
appeal. You can actually journey quite a lot of the island's
238 square miles (383 square kilometres) in a seven-day
break. Tracks are graded to suit all cyclists, from beginner
to seasoned pro. Delve into dense rainforest along mulch-
sawdust cycle paths that weave up-and-down hills or trace
the island's shoreline on an anti-clockwise loop. A round-

Photo: Javen466

island trip offers natural challenges for experienced riders, basic trails for beginners and single-track intermediate-level loops for advanced bikers with long but gradual uphills and steep, fast downhills.

The Soufrière to Vieux Fort trail is less gruelling, with plenty of time for a slow-paced pat of the pedals in order to admire the views of the island's dense, vine-tangled terrain and lesser-known root-riddled inner reaches. With its dormant volcano, St Lucia has rich, fertile soils that sprout with thickets of bloom-filled vegetation and bubbling sulphur springs. Trees, shrubs and towering palms characterise the landscape, but even in the barest patches you'll find nesting iguana, spindly trees that are home to rare birds and secret rugged sea caves. Cycling in Saint Lucia is an incredible way to experience Mother Nature's triumph because it is home to six single-island endemic bird species – the highest number of endemic birds in the Eastern Caribbean region. Cycle through wetlands and you'll be wowed by ducks, herons, sand pipers, plovers, egrets, gallinules, rails and other shorebirds and waterfowl. Choose a forest trail and you stand a real chance of spotting the brightly coloured Saint Lucia Parrot or the exotic Saint Lucia Black Finch, Saint Lucia Oriole, Saint Lucia Pewee and Saint Lucia Warbler fluttering among the trees.

For me, the eight miles (thirteen kilometres) of leafy bike trails lovingly carved out of the jungle that form the Tinker Trail are a favourite St Lucia challenge. This crowd-free path is blessed by magical birdsong and solitude. No roar of traffic. Just me, my bike and the sounds of nature. Due to the heat, the journey begins near Soufrière at dawn. It's hot and the island's south-west shoreline is usually shrouded in a steamy haze in the early hours. With panniers secured and sprockets, valves and spokes all checked, the Tinker Trail awaits. Named after legendary American Olympic cyclist David 'Tinker' Juarez, the trail is dubbed 'the sweetest in the Caribbean', but after navigating a tight series of skinny switchbacks along steep hills, you may wonder if you've misread 'sweet' for 'sweat'. The trail rises 1,000 feet (305 metres) from the expansive gardens of the Anse Chastanet beach resort in roughly a mile – no mean feat on a mountain bike. Set on 600 acres (243 hectares) of lush tropical rainforest bordering two beaches, this is St Lucia's premium beach resort, where upscale hotel suites on flawless sands provide million-dollar views. It's hard going and at times you'll end up carrying your bike over sheer climbs before settling back into the saddle, making weary riders all the more grateful for the visual stimulation of the scenery.

At the sign of the Tinker Trail's last steep jungle stretch, you may need to dig deep for an epic final push before juddering to a halt. Having survived one of the most challenging rides in the Caribbean, the reward is to ring Tinker's Bell victoriously, gasping at the jaw-dropping views over mango and breadfruit trees to the glittering Caribbean beyond. But remember, there's still the gut-wrenching, white-knuckle rollercoaster-style downhill ride home. If the uphill is tough, then the downhill is crazy: the trails slide around on a narrow strip that is running with moisture. Because you're pumped full of elation having made it to the top, there is a temptation to relax a bit on the tricky ride down, but this is risky. The trail is a skid fest and I was terrified of overdoing the speed on the descent and being thrown off into the trees. While the possibility of injury was a worry, it wasn't my main concern. It was the density of the foliage around me that scared me: close to the trail it is thick, thorny and spiky. Mongoose, possums and agouti hide out in this part of St Lucia and I also didn't fancy landing up face-to-face in the mud surrounded a pack of the island's feral jungle pigs. Time for the adrenaline to start seriously pumping …

Endurance level: Difficult

Tip: Treat yourself to a dip in the sea after this uphill slog – the salt water will ease the aches and pains.

Contacts:
St Lucia Tourist Board
www.saintluciauk.org

Bike St Lucia
www.bikestlucia.com

LA RUTA DE LOS CONQUISTADORES, COSTA RICA

This exciting multi-terrain 270-kilometre ride across Costa Rica is an inter-oceanic gem, slicing through bird-filled rainforest, volcanic slopes, coffee plantations and muddy backroads between the Pacific and Caribbean coasts. Each November, an ever-growing fleet of seasoned pros and mountain bike hard-men complete La Ruta de los Conquistadores (The Route of the Conquistadors) in just three days as part of the annual challenge that gives the ride its name. But there is no need to speed through such thrilling scenery. No need at all. For the route deserves your full attention, tracing the footsteps of 16th-century conqueror Juan de Cavallón, the Spanish chief conquistador. He famously slashed his way through densely knotted jungle with a machete, bravely fighting off wild animals and slaying the great eagles that tried to peck his eyes. Take note, riders. Take note.

At roughly the size of Switzerland, Costa Rica is home to an extraordinary array of natural wonder packed into a pocket size area of land. As one of the Top 20 countries in terms of biodiversity, it has over 500,000 species of flora and fauna, which represents nearly 4 per cent of all the species on planet earth – quite a feat for such a small country. Costa Rica, together with the land that is now Panama, formed a land-bridge connecting the North and South American continents around 5 million years ago, allowing a vast array of flora and fauna to mix. For cyclists, a downside of this wildlife-rich nation is that it is home to more than 300,000 bugs – a large proportion of which seem to lodge between my teeth.

Widely known as La Ruta, the race was conceived as a way of drawing the attention of the media to the importance of the continued conservation of flora and fauna. It began as an ecological hike following the paths of the Spanish Conquerors, Juan de Cavallon, Perafán de Ribera and Juan Vázquez de Coronado, during their explorations around 1653–1660, becoming a race, with a bike, in 1994. Román Urbina, a renowned athlete, adventurer and nominee for the mountain bike hall of fame, is the mastermind behind the mountain bike competition, launching it for fun. It was well subscribed, much enjoyed and drew international attention to Costa Rica rainforests and has been an annual fixture in the cycling calendar ever since.

La Ruta de los Conquistadores is renowned for pushing some of the world's strongest mountain bikers to their limits on one of the toughest, most beautiful courses on the planet. First staged in 1992, the race tests athletes with around 8,000

Photo: MongeNájera

metres (2,624 feet) of elevation gain and strong climate changes. The event is also open to amateurs, having a twelve-hour window to finish each stage. In a heart-warming gesture, the race begins on a Thursday, so that competitors have the Sunday to recover from taking three days to finish a route that took the Spanish conquistadors twenty years. Bikes rattle over rickety bridges that straddle swollen rivers and thunderous rapids. Where there isn't a bridge, riders will need to wade through the water holding their bikes high over their heads.

With more than 25 per cent of its land beautifully conserved (a quarter has National Park status), Costa Rica is the perfect place for an elongated mountain bike trail: crossing rivers, climbing rugged peaks and cutting through neck-high tall wild grass. Unlike on race day, there aren't any rescue trucks in the event you run out of steam on a gruelling ascent. You'll also need to carry plenty of water, food, bug spray, a first aid kit and a hammock, because there aren't Aid Stations located every 25 kilometres (16 miles) as there are when there are 500 competitors. However, just like on the race, you will find plenty of camaraderie and support if you join a small ride group. Riding La Ruta delivers a decent taste of all of Costa Rica's awe and wonder, primarily along energy-sapping red mud dirt roads.

In temperatures of 30–35°C, the altitude change riders experience on the first day is twelve metres (39 feet), to 650 metres (2,132 feet), to 1,201 metres (3,920 feet), to 490 metres (1,608 feet), finishing at 855 metres (2,805 feet) above sea level. Surfaces vary from mud, gravel and asphalt to dust and loose rocks. Beginning at the palm-scattered ocean-front of Jaco Beach on the west coast to Bonita Beach on the shores of the Caribbean, the road immediately shows who is boss. It climbs up. And up. And up and up and up. As a contestant in the annual challenge, you are faced with 3,000 metres (9,842 feet) of climbing on the first day alone. For many visiting riders, unused to the rainforest, the prospect of meeting a 60-kilogram (132-pound) giant rodent (capybara), tusk-gnashing peccary, hundreds of snakes, lurid green tree frogs and spiders the size of a tea tray is enough to get them moving – as fast as they can.

From Tres Ríos, located in the province of Cartago, the next section runs to Turrialba, also in Cartago – a 79-kilometre (49-mile) slog with an elevation gain of about 2,500 metres (8,200 feet). The altitude change is 1,291 metres (4,235 feet), to 3,025 metres (9,924 feet), to 607 metres (1,991 feet) above sea level. The climate is a drastic change from the previous section, due to the prevalence of wind and rain and temperatures that range from 5 to 8°C. Hypothermia is very real threat on this section, which begins with a fearsome climb of about 1,830 metres (6,000 feet) in near freezing conditions.

From here, La Ruta de los Conquistadores heads to Playa Bonita in the province of Limón over a distance of around 120 kilometres (75 miles) with an elevation gain of 800 metres (2,600 feet). A tropical wet climate is characterised by steamy temperatures of 35°C (or more) along a hot, muggy and humid section in which 65 per cent of the trail is mud. A series of climbs and downhills typifies the first 60 kilometres (97 miles), with the last half mainly flat but sticky – don't be fooled, despite the relatively small amount of climbing, this is a hard, long slog. Thankfully, the traditional finale to a trip along La Ruta de los Conquistadores is a dip in the Caribbean. Riding in is optional, but has been done.

Anyone following La Ruta is encouraged to follow eco-friendly practices regarding the disposal of rubbish, and using biodegradable detergents and oils. But after travelling through such natural splendour, you'll not want anything to muddy the memories of Costa Rica's magnificence.

Endurance level: Moderate–Difficult

Tip: Bugs biting? Do as the local cyclists do and rub lemon juice into exposed areas of skin for protection.

Contacts:
Essential Costa Rica
www.visitcostarica.com

Ruta de los Conquistadores
www.adventurerace.com

BOGOTÁ, COLOMBIA

Every week more than a million cyclists take over the busiest, biggest and most important streets of one of the most notoriously traffic-snarled metropolises in South America – Bogotá. Imagine, if you can, that happening in London, New York or Panama City? Exactly. There would be all sorts of chaos. Not so in Bogotá. A sure sign that truly incredible things can happen in a country where cyclists own the streets. For a good two decades, successive mayors of Bogotá have joined forces with various eco agencies, including Colombian think tank La Ciudad Verde ('Green City'). A whole host of initiatives have actively sought to end the city's love affair with the gas-guzzling car by making cycling and walking safer and sexier.

Much is owed to Antanas Mockus, who was undoubtedly Bogotá's most flamboyant and most progressive mayor. Holding office from 1995 to 1997 and again 2001 to 2003, Mockus – a philosopher, mathematician and former president of the National University of Colombia – employed his spirited intelligence to improve the quality of life in Bogotá. First several troupes of mime artists were allowed to roam the street and ridicule anyone who had parked illegally. Then, hordes of people holding over-sized 'thumbs up' signs made from foam applauded anyone seen acting with consideration: the teen helping the grandmother to cross the road safely; the truck driver respecting right of way; the housewife scooping up litter to pop it into a bin as she passes; and anyone leaving their car at home to travel the city by bike. Once some civic pride and social responsibility had been introduced, and citizens of Bogotá began to feel greater pride in their hometown, dozens of comedians were let loose city-wide to crack jokes and get the place smiling. Within a few years, a city that had once been a byword for the very worst in social ills had embraced a life-changing cycling tradition. Over 400 kilometres (248 miles) of cycle paths were built in Bogotá – one of the world's highest capital cities at 2,625 metres (861 feet) above sea level.

Today, two decades later, Colombia is a nation returned to peace following the drug wars and violent conflict of the past. Bogotá's traffic jams have eased too, since rules restricting the volume of cars has helped to clean up the city. The introduction of the world's first large-scale bus rapid transport system and a slew of pro-cycling policies, including car-free days and closing certain streets to cars on Sundays, have seen the average resident – who spends 22 days a year travelling in the city – save eight days per annum by simply switching to riding a bike. In status-obsessed South

American society, cycling is also a leveller: everyone is equal on a bicycle and there's been a unifying bond in Bogotá where there's a vast disparity in wealth. The poorest people live in the south, the middle class in the middle and the rich in the north; these different classes rarely mix, except on Sundays during the Ciclovia.

It's cool (chevre) to cycle in Bogotá today, and there's a thriving urban cycling culture, from women on bikes with shopping baskets and hip teens on day-glow BMXs to funky students riding ancient Dutch roadbikes and pro-cyclists racing around on featherlight carbon fibre. During the Sunday ride, from 7am to 2pm, more than 112 kilometres (70 miles) of city streets are gloriously traffic-free and around 1 million of Bogotá's 8 million inhabitants ride the Ciclovia in celebration. Colombia is now so evangelical about cycling, the buzz is spreading around the globe, from Los Angeles to Cape Town, Guadalajara to Rio de Janeiro. Cycling hasn't only changed Colombia, it is also changing the world.

To ride Bogotá is to discover a city that prides itself on loving the pedal. Students and lecturers journey by bike with books balanced on the handlebars, while deliverymen transport bags of fresh potatoes and boxes of mangoes along the designated bicycle routes (marked with stripes on the sidewalk). If you drive across Bogotá it will take at least 70 minutes – on a bicycle, it's a 30-minute trip.

Bogotá's dozens of bicycling clubs each has an individual bicycling leitmotif, be it wealthy amateur racers, leisurely cruisers, BMXers, all forms of mountain bikers and lovers of old classic bikes. You'll see them all as you careen through the steep, narrow cobblestone streets of old Bogotá – for the full thrill of the city, ride Carrera Séptima end to end, from Calle 126 in the north, down through the heart of the city, all the way to Calle 20 South, then circle back up along Carrera 15, completing the full north–south loop. Do it, of course, when the street is filled with cyclists, on a Sunday. Entire families are out together and there are plenty of grandmothers still pedalling the bikes they got when they were smooth-skinned teenagers. Sunday brings the street jugglers out on penny-farthings, as well as numerous clowns, musicians and costumed riders. When you reach the Plaza de Bolívar, take time to stop and study the monumental Catedral Primada de Colombia, Colombia's largest cathedral, built in 1823. Great swarms of cyclists are circling around the statue of Simón Bolívar with true two-wheeled passion.

Pedal power feels triumphant in a city roughly the same size as Greater London and there is no better way to get to know Bogotá than to sightsee in-the-saddle. Several special tour companies rent bikes and run group rides having briefed you on the route and checked panniers, sprockets, valves and spokes. One of the best is Bogotá Biking tour, an award-winning outfit, which runs small group rides for people who would prefer not to cycle solo.

Not in Bogotá on a Sunday? Then leave the fast-paced metropolitan centre behind and take the climbing route north-bound towards Colombia's breadbasket region: a picturesque rural patchwork of coffee, tobacco, cereal crops and farmland so resplendent in colour the locals call it *el tapiz* (the tapestry). Smooth, asphalted trails weave through a fertile landscape of fruit trees, vibrant blooms, gushing rivers and deep rocky gorges. Hens peck at scraps of corn by roadside cheese stalls, tethered horses graze by piles of pumpkins and sombrero-wearing herdsmen in grey woollen ponchos tend to goats on steep grassy banks. Colombia's national cycling team train along this route, so it boasts a fine Olympic pedigree. It is near-silent apart from the whir of free-spinning wheels and clicking gears of several-dozen bicycles passing through. Due to the high altitude, the locals describe Bogotá as being '2,600 metres closer to heaven', in reference to the capital's celestial characteristics. The pace may be punishing, and the air may be thin, but the message is clear in the city: Bogotá welcomes everyone, not just vehicles.

Endurance level: Easy–Moderate

Tip: Allow plenty of time to acclimatize to the city's high altitude – then slowly does it.

Contacts:
Bogotá Bike Tours
www.bogotabiketours.com

Colombia Bike Junkies
www.colombianbikejunkies.com

Colombia Tourist Board
www.colombia.travel

AFRICA

LUXOR, EGYPT

Imagine enjoying the freedom of hitting the open road in and around Luxor on the east bank of the Nile River in southern Egypt. As you pedal along at your own pace, with the warm desert winds around your ankles, a hot and stuffy coach packed with herded tourists passes by. The agony and envy on their faces is all too obvious. Luxor is on the site of ancient Thebes, the capital of the pharaohs during the 16th–11th centuries BC, at the height of their power. Homer is said to have described it as the 'City of the Hundred Gates' and for many years it ranked among the most important cities in the world as Ancient Egypt's centre of political, economic, religious and military life. Bordered by the desert, Luxor today runs lengthways along the Nile's east bank, with the royal tombs of the Valley of the Kings and the Valley of the Queens on the river's west bank.

Cycling in Egypt is fast-growing in popularity, as a transport choice, as a fitness craze and as an ecological initiative. Luxor's compact size makes it easy to navigate on bicycle. Once you've transferred from the International Airport, a twenty-minute jaunt by shuttle bus to the city centre, Luxor is basically a trio of main roads. Everything is located within a short distance of each other in around The Corniche, al-Mahatta and al-Karnak. Decent asphalt roads run through pretty tree-lined boulevards, busy tourist zones and roads to main transit areas, temples and hotels. It was here that Agatha Christie is said to have penned her classic work *Death on the Nile*. A bridge now links the east and west banks from a landing opposite the opulent Luxor Temple, an attractive, subtly lit building that glints after dark. Built during the New Kingdom, the temple is entered through a huge pylon built by Ramses II, with two of the original six statues representing the king on either side. There is also one of a pair of matching 25-metre (82-foot) granite obelisks: the other stands proud in the Place de la Concorde in Paris, a much photographed landmark.

Hired bikes are easy to find in Luxor: there are a good half-dozen rental shops. All tend to hire out the heavy single-

Photo: ianpudsey

geared Chinese models that are engineered to plod on forever. Low on speed, but high on durability, these battle-axes of the backroads always need a thorough pre-ride check – tyres, brakes, pedals, handlebars and padlock. Bikes are dirt cheap to hire for the day and you'll find the bike shops on the west bank slightly better value than those on the east bank. Some hotels organise rentals too. Luxor is best seen on bicycle and catching the ferry across The Nile is a breeze. When you need to leave your bike securely, someone will pop up to look after it for a small baksheesh (tip). Bikes come with a holder for a water bottle, and Luxor itself is flat, with all sites a short ride of the centre. You can't get lost – just head directly away from the river and you'll soon be at the Colossi of Memnon. The only arduous climb is the trail to the Valley of the Kings, which is a long ride uphill. The pay-off is the wind-in-your-hair freewheel down: a total rush.

To reach Luxor from Cairo, either fly or cycle out of the city. If you decide to do it by bike, leave early before the usual crazy traffic-rush starts. Travelling 500 kilometres (312 miles) to the south of Cairo through rural terrain means bidding the noisy polluted city centre farewell. After around 24 kilometres (fifteen miles), the gritty wind becomes fresher and cleaner. Then there are fewer and fewer horn-honking trucks. After about 48 kilometres (30 miles), the road continues to get quieter as you approach the sparsely populated countryside. Then to a desert landscape, empty apart from occasional industrial buildings – and this is how it stays. Beside you, never far away, is the mighty Nile River – the lifeblood of Egypt, past and present. There are plenty of overnight places to stay or pitch a tent. I opt for a hillside lodge, close to the hills on the outskirts of Beni Suef. From here, catch a train to Luxor, where cycling is enjoyed at a more genteel pace. If you can, splurge on First Class train tickets. The seats are spacious, the air conditioning works and the toilet has a working door. There are several flights of stairs between street level and many of the platforms, which is a hassle with a bike. However, bikes are secured and locked in the luggage hold with the luggage rack big enough to hold four panniers. You can do this journey overnight.

You can hire bicycles by the day (or by the week) with some form of ID. Go to the Dutch Bike Rental shop on Sheraton Street (next to the DHL parcel office on the east bank) for the best rental models – gears and parts are imported from Holland. You can also pick up maps here and hire a cycling Egyptologist to lead your private bike tour. Another good source of info is Cycle Egypt, the country's biggest group of cycling amateurs. As well as promoting cycling as a lifestyle choice and a sport, it also publicises all aspects of mountain cycling, cycling trips, events and races.

If you are unlucky enough to be stuck with a one-speed bike or a hotel rental, cycling uphill can be a source of frustration (and pain) because you can't change gears. To make things easier (presumably because they know some of the bikes are rubbish), taxi drivers ply their services at the bottom of the climb and offer to drive cyclists and their bikes up to the Valley of the Kings so that they can enjoy the downhill thrill. Main sights and intersections are well-marked. Cyclists get to see some of the less famous sites that a tour wouldn't cover, such as the Ramesseum and Medinet Habu. Be sure to take lots of water with you; it is sold at the main sights, but on sight of a pink-cheeked, sun-parched cycling tourist, the price inflates with an eye-watering mark up.

While you don't need to be a great sportsman or an Olympic cyclist to explore Luxor on a bike, you may well deserve a medal for surviving the sweatiness of the midday heat. It can be incredibly hot in Luxor, with average summer temperatures of 34°C, but at least you have a breeze on a bike. If you're unsure of cycling solo in high temperatures, you can always hire a cycling guide as a buddy. Luxor resident Mohamed Badwy knows Luxor's little-explored backcountry intimately. He can be booked by email: mohamed@badwytours.com.

Endurance level: Moderate–Difficult

Tip: Pick an extra-strong pair of sunglasses for this trip – the roads are exposed with very little shelter or shade.

Contacts:
Luxor Website
www.luxor.gov.eg

Egyptian Tourist Board
www.egypt.travel

KARURA FOREST, KENYA

Tucked in the midst of Nairobi's sweltering downtown business district, among the embassy buildings and corporate HQs, you'll find a 1,000-hectare (2,471-acre) pocket of green space: verdant, leafy and full of monkeys, exotic birds and colourful butterflies. Despite its close proximity to the urban sprawl, the Karura Forest Reserve is cool and spacious: a rare breath of air in a hot, dusty African capital. Established in 1932 and managed by the Kenya Forest Service, the forest has been fiercely protected against redevelopment by the Greenbelt Movement. Today, Kaurua Forest Reserve offers city-dwellers a blissful retreat from Nairobi's infamous car fumes and gridlocked traffic. Sheltered, shady, quiet, clean and oh-so-relaxing with the chirping melodies of birdsong the only distraction, the forest forms a sharp contrast with the rest of central Nairobi.

Cycles are available for hire to explore the jumble of way-marked trails that loop around waterfalls, sprouting bamboo, flower-filled marshlands, soaring trees and dozens of Mau Mau caves. These large overhanging rocks of huge historical importance were used for shielding freedom fighters from colonial forces during Kenya's 'Emergency Period' (1952–1960). Today, they are used as a place to prop your bike while you marvel at scuttling bush babies, snuffling porcupines, bush pigs and shy antelope.

The forest contains nearly all the 605 species of wildlife found in the region, including wild cats, monkeys, squirrels, hares, bats, monitor lizards, pythons, green snakes and around 200 species of birds. Of its avian species, the stand-outs are the majestic Ayres hawk-eagle and African crowned eagle, but you'll also find hornbills, owls, crested cranes, sparrows, doves and weavers. Ironically, vultures can be spotted – with their wrinkly heads, hooked beak and flappy-winged hop – by the incinerator formerly used by Central Bank of Kenya to burn old currency notes.

As you cycle through the Karura Forest, it is wise to keep a loose grip on the brake lever, ready to apply sudden pressure when antelopes decide to pop up in front of your speeding wheel. Silent cycles can inch through soft forests without scaring all the wildlife away and it isn't uncommon for porcupines and birds to cross the trail slowly and seemingly oblivious of anything approaching them at speed. I startled a red duiker, or rather it surprised me: a small antelope with a reddish unmarked coat, small neckless head and deep-

Photo: Ninaras

reddish-chestnut rump. A sign in the park states the speed limit is 40 kph – but I'm certain the wide-eyed red duiker violated this when he made his getaway.

At weekends, the park attracts legions of stressed-out urbanites keen to absorb the 'great outdoors' – the trails fill up with joggers, cyclists and walkers. Weekdays are extremely quiet. In the morning, it can be a place of solace: a peaceful spot to rest your soul and spirit. At lunchtime, picnickers scatter their blankets around the waterfall cascades, while ladies-who-lunch grab a table at the River Cafe nestled in among a forest clearing overlooking bird-filled pools. Cyclists ride the park all day long, arriving in the saddle or taking a rental model for a test around the outer trails (there's one of about fifteen kilometres [nine miles], another at approximately eight kilometres [four miles] and a four-kilometre [two-mile] stretch). Hiring a cycle for two hours costs about KSh500 (£4, as at 2016) at the Karura Forest and it is almost certainly the safest place to ride a bike in Nairobi. Monkeys swing in the trees as you pedal underneath, past wetlands scattered with waterfowl and croaking frogs. Paths are colour-coded for distance and direction, otherwise the forest feels like a secret hideaway waiting to be discovered. The toughest aspect is the altitude: Nairobi is 1,890 metres (5,971 feet) and cyclists in good shape for sea level are often surprised to suffer from heavy legs for the first couple of days. Forest trails are gentle with a few mild slopes that meander upwards under dangling creepers and swooping boughs.

The park opens at 8am and closes at 5pm and is best visited in the sunshine of the driest months (October to end of March) or in July and August when it is cool and cloudy. Avoid the wettest months April to June as the long rains turn the Karura Forest trails into a quagmire (the average annual rainfall in Karura is 930 millimetres/36 inches). You'll find the entrance to the park on Limuru Road next to the flag-strewn Belgian Embassy – there are three main entrance gates: Limuru Road, Kiambu Road and Old Kiambu Road. Frequent buses from the city centre serve Karura Forest, including numbers 11B, 106, 107, 108, 114 and 116. Or grab a taxi from the city centre (it should cost no more than KSh1,100).

Endurance level: Easy–Moderate

Tip: Rinse your cycling gloves out each day to prevent any bacteria build-up from sweat – there are zero places to buy replacements en route.

Contacts:
Friends of Karura Forest
www.friendsofkarura.org

Nairobi City Tourism
www.nairobicity.com

Kenya Forest Service
www.kenyaforestservice.org

NORTHERN TULI GAME RESERVE, BOTSWANA

The Northern Tuli Game Reserve is a truly spectacular north-eastern corner of Botswana. Spectacular landscapes, rich and varied wildlife and a host of historical, cultural and natural history attractions define its unique character.

Straddling the Shashe, Motloutse and Limpopo Rivers, which serve as natural boundaries with Zimbabwe and South Africa it covers more than 71,000 hectares (175,444 acres) of remarkably diverse habitat, including mophane bushland, riverine woodland and marshland punctuated by towering sandstone cliffs, basalt formations and unusually shaped kopjes. The Northern Tuli Game Reserve is also home to 48 species of mammals and over 350 species of birds, with an estimated 20,000 animals residing within its environs. Wildlife species include elephant, kudu, zebra, impala, duiker, wildebeest, waterbuck, steenbok and warthog. Large herds of eland – often not seen elsewhere in Botswana – are an awesome sight. All major predators, including lion, leopard, cheetah and hyena, are present. The birdlife is prolific and a bird-count of well over a hundred is doable in a single day.

Unlike other safari reserves, where the pace is sedentary, the Northern Tuli Game Reserve is aimed squarely at active encounters, especially cycling, hiking and horse-riding. There are also a number of opportunities to get involved in conservation and community-based projects, such as helping conservation staff research critical wildlife conservation issues – the Northern Tuli Game Reserve forms the heart of the proposed Shashe/Limpopo Trans-Frontier Conservation Area (TFCA). Its signatories – Botswana, Zimbabwe and South Africa – have agreed to cooperate to conserve and manage shared natural resources. Rich in biodiversity, the proposed TFCA will cover approximately 4,872 square kilometres (1,881 square miles) and will be one of the largest wildlife conservation areas in Southern Africa, with the Northern Tuli Game Reserve as its base.

If you're keen to cycle as part of a small group, Cycle Mashatu offers some excellent game-watching cycling tours, including the Mashatu Wilderness Trail. Situated between the Tuli Safari Area, a national park in Zimbabwe and the Mapungubwe National Park, a World Heritage Site in South Africa, Mashatu comprises 40 per cent of the Northern Tuli Game Reserve. Sharing unfenced borders with both the South African and Zimbabwean national parks, it is part of a vast cross-boundary wildlife conservation area protecting the substantial biodiversity of fauna and flora in this region. It is, without a doubt, Mashatu that most people conjure up when imagining the great wilderness areas in Africa. Mammoth open spaces, extraordinary creatures and sweeping, smogless skies offer beauty and tranquillity to visitors keen to have intimate contact with this remarkable landscape on two wheels.

Cyclists meet on the South African side at the Pont Drift Border Post to deal with the border formalities and bike preparations together, then the wilderness adventures begin. An exhilarating fifteen-kilometre (nine-mile) ride to the camp is rewarding by chilled drinks, a hot bucket shower and a wholesome dinner of lip-smacking chicken cooked over an open fire. Camps are low-impact but fully equipped and don't skimp on comfort out in the midst of the wild African bush.

When dawn arrives, there is plenty of fresh brewed coffee and a breakfast of eggs, fruit and bread. Then it is off on our bikes for a fun 25-kilometre (15-mile) ride across rocky outcrops, sandy riverbeds and dusty open plains. After a fire-roasted fish lunch, and an afternoon trek along bushland trails, we enjoy a sundowner on a table-top plateau – the sheer magic of the deep baronial hues of the sunset make my goose bumps tingle.

Cycle out to Mapungubwe Hill, site of a prosperous Iron Age city almost 1,000 years old on the banks of the Limpopo

Photo: Sjoberth

River. Ruled by a king of the Leopard Kopje people, Mapungubwe had extensive trade networks that reached as far as Egypt, India and China. Accessible via two very steep and narrow paths that twist their way to the summit, Mapungubwe was a highly developed civilisation with unique arts – including pottery and jewellery – of a superior craftsmanship and quality. Backdropped by a breathtaking landscape of woodlands, riverine forests and sandstone formations, the area around Mapungubwe Hill is rich in wildlife, including white rhino, elephant, giraffe, gemsbok, eland, lion, leopard and hyena.

Venture into the quaint village of Motlhabaneng to spend a morning with the village chief to learn about the settlement's history. Watch local children dance in traditional clothing and local artisans hand-weave baskets with nimble proficiency. Ancient rock paintings, almost certainly done by Southern Africa's original inhabitants, the San, can also be seen on the outskirts of Motlhabaneng. The paintings depict people, animals, hunting scenes and mythological creatures, part of the San's complex cosmology and belief system.

To make the most of the best cycling weather, try to avoid the rainy season from December to April. Almost all of the main roads in Botswana boast a decent grade of asphalt surfacing. With very few hills, the country is fairly flat, with only a couple of tough climbs, so there is ample opportunity to spot big mammals. Botswana is a pachyderm paradise: you'll regularly hear the rumbles and calls of elephants as you pedal over the plains. You'll never grow used to seeing them by the side of the country's easy-to-navigate highways – African elephants are the largest of all land animals, with adult males weighing in between 1,800 and 6,300 kilograms (two and seven tons/4,000 and 14,000 pounds). Standing at a height of well over three metres (nine feet), with wrinkled, textured folds of skin and a trunk with more than 100,000 muscles and tendons, elephants are blessed with an acutely sensitive sense of smell and hearing. A sizeable mouth has a total of 26 teeth, including two upper incisors (tusks), twelve premolars and twelve huge molars the size of house-bricks – a scary armoury. As you cycle in Botswana, you'll hear them wheezing, gasping, snorting, their sparse hairs twitching and ears flapping. On wide open country roads with infrequent traffic, at times you are so close to grazing elephants you can almost feel their breath as you pass.

Endurance level: Easy–Moderate

Tip: This ride is wild and wonderful – if you're lucky you'll see elephants wandering across the highway!

Contacts:
Botswana Tourist Board
www.botswanatourism.co.bw

Cycle Mashatu
www.mtbsafaris.com

African Bikers
www.africanbikers.com